Discover the Eastern Adirondacks

Four-Season Adventures near
Lake George, Pharaoh Lake and Beyond

Discover the Eastern Adirondacks

Four-Season Adventures near
Lake George, Pharaoh Lake and Beyond

Barbara McMartin

with the assistance of Edythe Robbins

A revised edition of *Guide to the Eastern Adirondacks*

Backcountry Publications
Woodstock, Vermont

An Invitation to the Reader
Over time trails can be rerouted and signs and landmarks altered. If you find that changes
have occurred on the routes described in this book, please let me know so that corrections
may be made in future editions. The author and publisher also welcome other comments
and suggestions. Address all correspondence to:

Editor
Discover the Adirondacks Series
Backcountry Publications
P.O. Box 175
Woodstock, VT 05091

Published by Backcountry Publications, Inc.
Woodstock, Vermont 05091
Printed in the United States of America by McNaughton & Gunn
Typesetting by The Sant Bani Press

Series design by Leslie Fry
Layout by Barbara McMartin
Maps by Richard Widhu

Photograph Credits
Barbara McMartin: 10, 40, 50, 111, 120, 132, 144, 158, 168, 179, 183, 187, 189, 192, 197,
202, 214
Lawrence King: 2, 18, 24, 77, 80, 88, 95, 113, 163, 171, 172
Edythe Robbins: cover, 32, 46, 56, 124, 128, 149, 152, 155, 177
William A. White: 73
W. Alec Reid: 211

Photographs
Cover: *Split Rock Bay on Pharaoh Lake*
Page ii: *Winter on Catamount Mountain*

Acknowledgments

THIS WORK BEGAN as a project of the Glens Falls Chapter of the Adirondack Mountain Club (ADK). For eighteen months, members organized trail research and recorded trail mileages and information. Their work still constitutes the basis for this guide and particular thanks are due Lilian Bull, Malcolm Archard, Edythe Robbins, Laura Meade, Gary Klee, Robert Kirker, Patricia Collier, Ruth Hadley, Douglas MacIntosh, Eileen Keegan, and James Cooper. Special thanks are due ADK for releasing the copyright to the guide so that it could be reissued in this revised edition as part of the Discover series. This series preserves the original format of the guide—the bushwhacks, the historical background, and all the information designed to swell the hiker's enthusiasm for the region.

I enjoyed many walks with those ADKers as I researched the area for the guide.

Edythe Robbins has done most of the trail checking needed to update the revised edition and has added new material. William M. White, James Spring, Lawrence and Maryde King also checked trails and added information on new bushwhacks. Lawrence King wrote the sections on Catamount and Barton High Cliffs.

Several people have written with new information on areas covered, exciting tidbits on new places to go, new caves and cliffs to explore. Suggestions from Robert Carroll, Jr., Herbert McAneny, Ken Smith, and Steve Etkind have been incorporated in the revised edition. Department of Environmental Conservation (DEC) Rangers Howard Lashway, Bob Morris, William Houck, Lance Killemeier, and James White all gave helpful information.

Historical background is enriched because of the help of Elsa Kny Steinback, Pamela Vogel, Robert Kirker, Warren Lee, William Casselman, Helen Persons, Barbara Germaine, and Clifton West.

My husband, W. Alec Reid, printed the photographs for the new edition, pictures that were taken by Edythe Robbins, Lawrence King, and myself.

Contents

Introduction

THIS GUIDE COVERS all the state land east of the Northway and south of the Moriah-North Hudson Road, which lies between Northway Exits 29 and 30. As you drive along the Northway, you can see a few of the lakes and peaks, Pharaoh and Buck Mountain, Schroon Lake and Lake George, for instance. But this view does not give you a clue to the wonderful hiking trails contained in the Pharaoh Lake Wilderness and the Lake George Wild Forest. Here you will find the best trail network in the Adirondacks—best in terms of interesting destinations, best in terms of design and maintenance. Within the area you will find some of the Adirondacks' best marked trails, routes that appeal to inexperienced hikers.

More experienced hikers will discover bushwhacks that range from the very easy to the very challenging. There is a network of old trails and bushwhacks in the Hammond Pond Wild Forest, which shares much in common with the Pharaoh Lake area—everything but the latter's popularity. Snowmobile trails south of Brant Lake make excellent ski trails. There are wonderful cross-country ski trips and exciting snowshoe bushwhacks throughout. Three new bushwhacks have been added to this revised edition, and one of them is among the Adirondack's best kept and more unusual secrets.

Although Lake George, the Adirondack's most beautiful lake, is a well-used recreation area, the routes in this guide will allow you to enjoy the remaining pristine charms of its mountainous shores.

As you walk over other parts of this region, you will find much of it is also already well known, but this guide will point you to the quieter parts. There are nearly three dozen peaks with views from windswept rocky summits, bared long ago by fires. There are twice as many ponds and lakes, almost all with attractive rock ledges along parts of their shores.

Some of the region's forests have been recovering from the disturbance of logging and fires for nearly a century and a half. Towering pines and hemlocks rival the virgin forests of the northwestern Adirondacks. This resemblance to virgin forests is enhanced by unpolluted, sparkling clear waters, and remote and quiet places of serene beauty. Everywhere, forests, marshes, and numerous bodies of water make this a gentle wilderness—inviting to all.

Barton High Cliffs

How to Use the "Discover" Guides

The regional guides in the *Discover the Adirondacks* series will tell you enough about each area so that you can enjoy it in many different ways at any time of year. Each guide will acquaint you with that region's access roads and trailheads, its trails and unmarked paths, some bushwhack routes and canoe trips, and its best picnic spots, campsites, and ski-touring routes. At the same time, the guides will introduce you to valleys, mountains, cliffs, scenic views, lakes, streams, and a myriad of other natural features.

Some of the destinations are within walking distance of the major highways that ring the areas, while others are miles deep into the wilderness. Each description will enable you to determine the best excursion for you and to enjoy the natural features you will pass, whether you are on a summer day hike or a winter ski-touring trek. The sections are grouped in chapters according to their access points. Each chapter contains a brief introduction to that area's history and the old settlements and industries that have all but disappeared into wilderness. Throughout the guides you will find accounts of the geological forces that shaped features of the land. Unusual wildflowers and forest stands also will be noted.

It is our hope that you will find this guide not only an invitation to know and enjoy the woods but a companion for all your adventures there.

MAPS AND NOMENCLATURE

The Adirondack Atlas, a map published by City Street Directory of Poughkeepsie, New York, is the best reference for town roads, and it has the added advantage of identifying state land. In spite of the fact that it has not been updated to show recent acquisitions, this is a valuable aid in the eastern region where public and private lands are so intricately mixed.

This guide contains maps that show all the routes mentioned, and these are adequate for the marked trails. You may still want to carry the USGS topographic quadrangle sheets for the region, and you ought to have them for the more difficult bushwhacks. The maps used include 7.5-minute series Lake George, Putnam Mountain, Bolton Landing, Shelving Rock, Whitehall, Chestertown, Brant Lake, Silver Bay, Putnam, Ticonderoga, Pharaoh Mountain, Graphite, Eagle Lake, and Paradox Lake, and the 15-minute series for Glens Falls, Bolton Landing, Lake Luzerne, and Paradox Lake.

The 15-minute maps are reproduced in the same scale, 1" = 1 mile. The 7.5-minute maps are uniformly reduced by 62 percent. *Note carefully this change in scale.* The scale is given on the reproduced maps and this percentage was chosen to give the greatest possible details as well as coverage.

Maps are available locally in many sporting stores. You can order maps from USGS Map Distribution Branch, Box 25286, Denver Federal Center, Denver, CO 80225. Maps are currently more easily obtained from a private source, Timely Discount Maps. You can call them at 1-800-821-7609; with your credit card number they will ship maps within a week.

The guide uses the spelling given in the USGS but local variations are noted.

DISTANCE AND TIME

Distance along the routes is measured from the USGS survey maps and is accurate to within ten percent. Few hikers gauge distance accurately even on well-defined trails. Distance is a variable factor in comparing routes along trails, paths, or bushwhacks.

Time is given as an additional gauge for the length of routes. This provides a better understanding of the difficulty of the terrain, the change of elevation, and the problems of finding a suitable course. Average time for walking trails is 2 miles an hour, 3 miles if the way is level and well defined; for paths, 1 ½ to 2 miles an hour; and for bushwhacks, 1 mile an hour.

Summaries for distance, time, and vertical rise are given with the title of each section describing a trail or path. These distances and times are for *one way only*, unless otherwise stated.

TYPES OF ROUTES

Each section of this guide generally describes a route or a place. Included in the descriptions are such basic information as the suitability for different levels of woods experience, walking (or skiing, paddling, and climbing) times, distances, directions to the access, and, of course, directions along the route itself. The following definitions clarify the terms used in this book.

A route is considered a *trail* if it is so designated by the New York State Department of Environmental Conservation (DEC). This means the trail is routinely cleared by DEC or volunteer groups and adequately marked with official DEC disks. *Blue disks* generally indicate major north-south routes, *red disks* indicate east-west routes, and *yellow disks* indicate side trails. This scheme is not, however, applied consistently throughout the Adirondacks.

Some trails have been marked for *cross-country skiing*, and new *pale yellow disks with a skier* are used. *Large orange disks* indicate *snowmobile trails*, which are limited to some portions of Wild Forest Areas. Snowmobiles are permitted on them in winter when there is sufficient snow cover. Many snowmobile trails on the interior are not heavily used and can be shared by those on cross-country skis as long as the skier is cautious. Hikers can enjoy both ski and snowmobile trails.

A *path* is an informal and unmarked route with a clearly defined foot tread. These traditional routes, worn by fishermen and hunters to favorite spots, are great for hiking. A path, however, is not necessarily kept open, and fallen trees and new growth sometimes obliterate its course. The paths that cross wet meadows or open fields often become concealed by lush growth. You should always carry a map and compass when you are following an unmarked path and you should keep track of your location.

There is a safe prescription for walking paths. In a group of three or more hikers, stringing out along a narrow path will permit the leader to scout until the path disappears, at which point at least one member of the party should still be standing on an obvious part of the path. If that hiker remains standing while those in front range out to find the path, the whole group can continue safely after a matter of moments.

Hikers in the north country often use the term *bushwhack* to describe an uncharted and unmarked trip. Sometimes bushwhacking literally means pushing brush aside, but it usually connotes a variety of cross-country walks.

Bushwhacks are an important part of this regional guide series because of the shortage of marked trails throughout much of the Adirondack Park and the abundance of little-known and highly desirable destinations for which no visible routes exist. Although experienced bushwhackers may reach these destinations with not much more help than the knowledge of their location, I think most hikers will appreciate these simple descriptions that point out the easiest and most interesting routes and the possible pitfalls. In general, descriptions for bushwhacks are less detailed than those for paths or trails; it is assumed that those who bushwhack have a greater knowledge of the woods than those who walk marked routes.

Bushwhack is defined as any trip on which you make your way through the woods without a trail, path, or the visible foot tread of other hikers and without markings, signs, or blazes. It also means you will make your way by following a route chosen on a contour map, aided by a compass, using streambeds, valleys, abandoned roads, and obvious ridges as guides. Most bushwhacks require navigating by both contour map and compass, and an understanding of the terrain.

Bushwhack distances are not given in precise tenths of a mile. They are estimates representing the shortest distance one could travel between points.

This reinforces the fact that each hiker's cross-country route will be different, yielding different mileages.

A bushwhack is said to be *easy* if the route is along a stream, a lakeshore, a reasonably obvious abandoned roadway, or some similarly well-defined feature. A short route to the summit of a hill or a small mountain can often be easy. A bushwhack is termed *moderate* if a simple route can be defined on a contour map and followed with the aid of a compass. Previous experience is necessary. A bushwhack is rated *difficult* if it entails a complex route, necessitating advanced knowledge of navigation by compass and reading contour maps and land features.

Compass directions for bushwhacks are given in degrees from magnetic north, a phrase abbreviated here to *degrees magnetic*.

The guide occasionally refers to old *blazed* lines or trails. The word "blaze" comes from the French *blesser* and means to cut or wound. Early loggers and settlers made deep slashes in good-sized trees with an axe to mark property lines and trails. Later, hunters and fishermen often made slashes with knives and, though they are not as deep as axe cuts, they too can still be seen. Following an old blazed path for miles in dense woods is often a challenging but good way to reach a trailless destination. Remember, though, that it is now, and has been for many years, illegal to deface trees in the Forest Preserve in this manner.

You may see *yellow paint daubs on a line of trees*. These lines usually indicate the boundary between private and public lands. Individuals have also used different colors of paint to mark informal routes from time to time. Although it is not legal to mark trails on state land, this guide does refer to such informally marked paths.

All *vehicular traffic*, except snowmobiles on their designated trails, is *prohibited* in the Forest Preserve. There are some town roads or roads that lead to private inholdings on which vehicular use is permitted. These roads are described in the guides, and soon the DEC will start marking those old roads that are open to vehicles. Most old roads referred to in the guides are town or logging roads that were abandoned when the land around them became part of the Forest Preserve. Now they are routes for hikers, not for vehicles.

There has been an increase in the use of three- and four-wheeled off-road vehicles, even on trails where such use is not permitted. New laws will stop this in the Forest Preserve and make sure that some of the old roads remain attractive hiking routes.

Cables have been placed across many streams by hunters and other sportsmen to help them cross in high water. The legality of this practice has been challenged. Some may be quite safe to use, others are certainly questionable. Using them is not a recommended practice, so when this guide mentions crossing streams to reach some of the hikes, you are urged to do so only when a boat can be used or in low water when you can wade across.

The *beginning of each section describing a trail* gives a summary of the distance, time, and elevation change for the trail. For unmarked routes, such information is given only within the text of each section—partly to allow for the great variations in the way hikers approach an unmarked route, and partly to emphasize the difficulty of those routes.

Protecting the Land

Most of the land described in these guides is in the *Forest Preserve,* land set aside a century ago, where no trees may be cut. All of it is open to the public. The *Adirondack Park Agency* has responsibility for the Wilderness, Primitive, and Wild Forest guidelines that govern use of the Forest Preserve. Care and custody of these state lands is left to the Department of Environmental Conservation, which is in the process of producing Unit Management Plans for the roughly 130 separate Forest Preserve areas.

Camping is permitted throughout the public lands except at elevations above 4000 feet and within 150 feet of water or 100 feet of trails. In certain fragile areas, camping is restricted to specific locations, and the state is using a new No Camping disk to mark fragile spots. *Permits* for camping on state lands are needed only for stays that exceed three days or for groups of more than ten campers. Permits can be obtained from the local rangers, who are listed in the area phone books under New York State Department of Environmental Conservation.

Only dead and downed wood can be used for *campfires.* Build fires only when absolutely necessary; carry a small stove for cooking. Build fires at designated fire rings or on rocks or gravelly soil. Fire is dangerous and can travel rapidly through the duff or organic soil, burning roots and spreading through the forest. Douse fires with water, and be sure they are completely out and cold before you leave.

Private lands are generally not open to the public, though some individuals have granted public access across their land to state land. It is always wise to ask before crossing private lands. Be very respectful of private landowners so that public access will continue to be granted. Never enter private lands that have been posted unless you have the owner's permission. Unless the text expressly identifies an area as state-owned Forest Preserve or private land whose owner permits unrestricted public passage, the inclusion of a walk description in this guide does not imply public right-of-way.

Burn combustible trash and carry out everything else.

Most *wildflowers and ferns* mentioned in the text are protected by law. Do not pick them or try to transplant them.

Safety in the Woods

It is best *not to walk alone.* Make sure someone knows where you are heading and when you are expected back.

Carry water or other liquids with you. Not only are the mountains dry, but the recent spread of *Giardia* makes many streams suspect. I have an aluminum fuel bottle especially for carrying water; it is virtually indestructible and has a deep screw that prevents leaking.

Carry a small *day pack* with insect repellent, flashlight, first aid kit, emergency food rations, waterproof matches, jackknife, whistle, rain gear, and a wool sweater, even for summer hiking. Wear layers of wool and waterproof clothing in winter and carry an extra sweater and socks. If you plan to camp, consult a good outfitter or a camping organization for the essentials. Better yet, make your first few trips with an experienced leader or with a group.

Always carry a *map and compass.* You may also want to carry an altimeter to judge your progress on bushwhack climbs.

Wear *glasses* when bushwhacking. The risk to your eyes of a small protruding branch makes this a necessity.

Carry *binoculars* for birding as well as for viewing distant peaks.

Use great care near the *edges of cliffs* and when *crossing streams* by hopping rocks in the streambed. Never bushwhack unless you have gained a measure of woods experience. If you are a novice in the out-of-doors, join a hiking group or hire the services of one of the many outfitters in the north country. As you get to know the land, you can progress from the standard trails to the more difficult and more satisfyingly remote routes. Then you will really begin to discover the Adirondacks.

Creek on Five Mile Mountain

Lake George

LAKE GEORGE HAS been the queen of Adirondack resorts since 1869 when regular stage coaches started carrying visitors along the plank road from the train station at Fort Edward. Lake George Village at the head of the lake was originally named Caldwell. The Fort William Henry Hotel, a marvel of arcaded porches, promenades, and boardwalks surrounding the massive six story structure, was built here in 1855. The view from its porch was of the lake and the encircling mountains. This is only one of the many vistas that helped Lake George earn the reputation as the prettiest of all the Adirondack lakes.

The lake was christened Lac du St. Sacrement by Father Isaac Jogues, the first white man to visit it. He traveled the length of the lake in 1646 on his way to the Mohawk River and martyrdom at the hands of the Mohawk Indians. In 1755 General William Johnson renamed it Lake George to honor his king, George II, and claim the territory for him. From the French and Indian War through the War of 1812, Lake George was the scene of a sequence of battles and skirmishes.

The history of the forts at Lake George and the battles that took place along its shores is best left to histories or a visit to the reconstructed Fort William Henry. But every walk you take in the historic hills that rim the lake will be the richer if you do take time to bone up on the past.

The lake occupies a deep fault valley as old as the mountains that form the Adirondacks. It was given its modern shape when glaciers sculpted its steep shore, scraping the mountains into precipitous faces. The lake probably had two predecessors. The glacial thrust deposited a layer of gravel and sand at the southern end, blocked an outlet south, and raised the level of the lake until a new outlet was formed at the north. The southern outlet is now a broad sand beach, today's Million Dollar Beach, the glory of Lake George Village.

A second flow north through Trout Brook was similarly blocked, and the thrust of the glacier broke the pass between two ancient lakes, leaving only the island-studded Narrows where the separation had been. The lake receives little surface drainage, which accounts for its extraordinarily clear water.

In addition to the public bathing beaches, you will find two state areas, the Fort George Battleground Park and the Hearthstone Point Campsite, both near the south end of Lake George. There is no better way to discover Lake George than a lake trip on one of the excursion boats. They leave from the south end of the lake on regular schedules throughout the summer months. You will want to begin your introduction to the lake with a visit to two of its southern mountains. Both Prospect and Buck Mountains have excellent hiking trails, and a first class highway will take you to Prospect's summit for a first glimpse of the country covered by this guide.

1 Prospect Mountain
An introduction by automobile

Prospect Mountain is proof that you do not need high elevation for a great view. By Adirondack standards, its 2030-foot height is almost insignificant. Many of the mountain valleys from which the "nobler" mountains spring are as high as Prospect's summit. Its summit is only two-fifths the height of the Adirondack's tallest peak, Mount Marcy. That peak, forty-eight miles distant, makes up a part of the amazing panorama from Prospect's summit.

Early visitors to the lake had as much appreciation for the surprising view from Prospect as do modern hikers. In the style of nineteenth century vacationing, a hotel was built on the summit. A fire in 1880 destroyed the first 1877 structure, but it was quickly rebuilt. An incline railway was constructed in 1895 to bring excursioners to the hotel's restaurant and dance hall. The railway lasted only seven years, though remains of its bullwheel and support foundations can still be seen on the mountain. The second hotel was finally dismantled in 1932 after the state had acquired the mountain property.

One of your first impressions of a trip up the mountain is sure to be the way in which trees and shrubs are finally beginning to regrow and recover the summit, which was once cleared to give the best views in all directions. The cover does little to protect the windswept summit, though, and jackets are often needed on even the warmest days.

Prospect Mountain Memorial Highway is maintained by the New York State Department of Environmental Conservation (DEC). The road leaves NY 9 between Exits 21 and 22 of the Northway. A fee of $2.25 is charged for each passenger vehicle, no matter the number of its occupants. Three turnouts from the highway offer differing vantages: At the first turnout, look for a red-marked trail leading from the southern corner of the parking

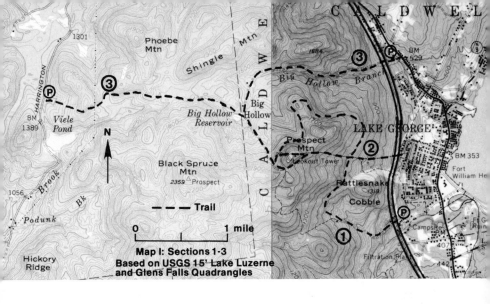

Map I: Sections 1-3
Based on USGS 15' Lake Luzerne
and Glens Falls Quadrangles

lot. In an easy-to-moderate climb of no more than 0.2 mile, it leads to a rocky outcrop called Rattlesnake Cobble. (It is the prominent little peak that looms up straight ahead when you pass Exit 21 going north on the Northway.) From its ledges there are views northeast over Lake George and the village. From here, a short bushwhack south over the ridge brings you to more open rocks and a nice view of the south end of the lake to Glens Falls. The second turnout also has views of the southern end of Lake George.

Some days you can drive directly to the summit, but if the weather is exceptionally clear, crowds limit parking to a large lot below the summit knob. From here a short climb or a transfer via free viewmobiles will take you to the summit with its picnic tables and special view spots.

One view spot is on the rock base that supports the unused fire tower. From it you can easily see Mount Marcy to the north; Gore Mountain to the northwest; Killington in Vermont; Equinox, thirty-three miles distant in Vermont; a portion of the Hudson River; the towers of the Empire State Mall, fifty-two miles away; and, on a very clear day, the tops of distant Catskill peaks, eighty miles to the south-southeast.

From another vantage at the top of the old incline railway you can see a portion of the Narrows of Lake George with Buck Mountain ranging to the south. Several peaks in Vermont can be identified, as well as many of the cluster that constitutes the High Peaks of the Adirondacks. Among the closer hills you should note Cat Mountain, distinguished by its cliffs, a little east of north. Just west of north lies Hoffman, a hulk that will loom distinctively when viewed from some of the northern peaks in this guide.

2 Prospect Mountain Foot Trail from the East
Hiking
2 miles, 1¾ hours, 1650-foot vertical rise

The trail on the east side of Prospect Mountain provides an excellent hike to the summit. The best time for a hike would be a clear day in fall or spring, the time to avoid the tourists.

The trailhead is on Smith Street in Lake George Village, at a stairway that leads up and over the Northway. Smith Street is parallel to the Northway and to NY 9 and can be reached by turning west from NY 9 onto Montcalm Street. Go five blocks to Cooper Street, turn right one block to West Street, and then left one block to Smith Street where you again turn left.

The first third of the ascent, the trail follows the rocky bed of the inclined railway. After crossing the toll road, the ascent becomes markedly steeper, with frequent rock outcrops and views to entice the hiker. When the trail reaches the toll road once more, you turn right on the road, go about seventy-five feet up it, and turn left into the picnic area.

3 Prospect Mountain via the Snowmobile Trail
Hiking, cross-country skiing
7 miles, 4 hours, 1650-foot vertical rise

A third approach to the summit of Prospect Mountain can be made via a snowmobile trail, which also offers a through trek from the east across the northern flanks of the mountain to its western side. The eastern trailhead is reached from Northway Exit 22. Go north from the exit on NY 9 for 0.5 mile until you see the Lake George Garage on your right. Turn left here on a dead end road and go 0.3 mile to the end of that road, just before culverts under the Northway. There is room here for a number of cars to park.

The western terminus of this trek is a fairly large parking area just a two-minute walk off Harrington Hill Road. To find that trailhead, take Northway Exit 23 and head toward Warrensburg. Turn left over the Schroon River and quickly turn left again. You are now heading south on County Route 12, which is Harrington Road. Just before Viele Pond, about 4 miles south, you will see a dirt road heading east. That leads to the trailhead. The route is exceptionally lovely in fall when the colors in Stewart Brook are at their height.

You start the climb by crossing under the Northway through the culverts and walking along a roadway marked with orange snowmobile trail disks. The roadway follows Old Hollow Brook, which is on your left. After a short walk through a hemlock grove, you reach an intersection, at 0.3 mile. The way left leads quickly to a small reservoir, a pretty, but often littered spot. The right fork continues west and up beside the brook, which is in a deep depression between two ridges. Your route is on the flank of the north ridge overlooking the brook. Here, stately hemlock border the road.

You leave the brook, and the north ridge becomes more gradual at just over 1 mile. At 1.4 miles you pass a turnout on the right where logs are piled. At 1.8 miles you reach an intersection where the trail or roadway forks right toward Harrington Hill Road.

To climb to the summit of Prospect Mountain, you take the left fork and shortly beyond the intersection you see a decrepit iron gate. The roadway begins to climb once more, this time through deciduous forests, and heads south. After a twenty-minute walk from the intersection, you reach the parking area on Prospect Mountain. The 2.8 miles from the trailhead requires an hour and fifteen minutes.

As you head across the parking area toward the walkway to the summit, you can enjoy views that stretch from the eastern side of Lake George to the distant mountains of Vermont. The paved walkway is to the left of the parking area. On the left as you climb, you look out toward Harrington Hill, Crane Mountain, Gore, Hadley, Roundtop, and Baldhead mountains. In another minute you are at the foot of the stairs that look directly up to the fire tower. You reach the old incline railway overlook at 3 miles.

To continue on the snowmobile trail, go back 1.2 miles to the trail intersection. Here, 4.2 miles into your trek, head left, west. The roadway, along which the trail is routed from the intersection to the western trailhead, would make an excellent cross-country ski route. You pass a swamp on your right at 4.6 miles and at 5.8 miles reach an unmarked intersection. The way right leads north to private lands and eventually to Harrington Hill Road. You want the left fork, which is actually straight ahead from the intersection. You cross under the high tension wires and walk up a gentle hill to a crest, just short of 6.2 miles.

The roadway starts sharply downhill beyond the crest and arrives at the parking area at 6.85 miles. Harrington Hill Road is 0.15 miles away.

Buck Mountain

4 Buck Mountain from the West

Hiking, snowshoeing, horseback riding
3.3 miles, 2½ hours, 2000-foot vertical rise

Buck Mountain rises steeply from the deepest part of Lake George, near the southern end of the range that forms the lake's eastern shore. A series of fault lines, defining shelves, edges the western slopes of the mountain, echoing the fault lines of the lake itself.

The round trip should take no more than four hours, and the views from the open summit are ample reward for the 2000-foot climb to the 2334-foot summit. West of south lies Lake George Village. Crane Mountain is due west, and Pharaoh Mountain lies due north. Between these mountains, on the horizon, you can spot Snowy, whose jagged knob distinguishes it even at a distance of forty-three miles; Gore Mountain, with its ski slopes; and the truncated top of Blue Mountain. On the distant horizon the Giant sits on the right of Pharaoh, and the cluster of High Peaks, which includes Dix and Marcy, is seen to the left of Pharaoh.

East of north, beyond Little Buck Mountain, lies Sleeping Beauty, with the wooded summit ridge of Erebus to the left, west, of it, and Black Mountain's summit barely visible above. To the east from a vantage on the east side below the summit, there are fine views of the Champlain Valley and the Green Mountains beyond.

The trailhead, called Pilot Knob, is south of Pilot Knob Point. From Northway Exit 20, head north on NY 9, east on NY 149 (known locally as the Farm-to-Market Road), and then north on NY 9L. At Katskill Bay, 7 miles north of NY 149, turn right where a sign states, "Pilot Knob, 4 miles." The trailhead for Buck Mountain is on the east side of that road, 3.3 miles from the intersection.

The trail up Buck Mountain begins along an abandoned roadway marked with yellow hiking disks and blue horse trail markers. The way is level through a hemlock bog to a hardwood forest. Several abandoned logging roads intersect the trail; you stay right at the first and left at 0.3 mile where the trail meets a second roadway. (The way right is described in section 5.)

The trail drops only slightly before soon crossing Butternut Brook, and just beyond there is a third intersection where you stay right. There is a picnic table beside the brook just at the point the trail pulls away from the deep valley of the brook to climb the hemlock covered slopes.

You head south of east, high above the left bank of Butternut Brook, with steep rock ledges above on your left. One cannot help but admire the way this trail with its rock base was built into the hillside. After a half hour of walking, at about 1.2 miles, you have climbed high enough to find a minor opening with a view of Pilot Knob Mountain to the south. The clearing here is edged with stone fences, remnants of farming days.

In a few minutes more, at 1.5 miles, you cross a stream with a waterfall. The stream is flowing south to join Butternut Brook. Immediately beyond it you reach an intersection with a sign pointing left, 1.8 miles to the summit. The way straight, or right, leads to Hogtown, section 7.

The left trail, now in a deep depression with high banks, begins to climb a gradual route along gentle switchbacks. After a zigzag, the route turns north, then northwest, returning to continue closer to the stream. A log road joins from the left as the trail swings sharply right and uphill. Farther uphill you pass a spring that is piped onto the trail, gradually crossing it to join the stream. The summit is dry, so be sure you have water. This is your last opportunity.

By this time, the trees are considerably smaller with lots of birch. Even with the switchbacks, the climb is noticeable, and you may spend as much as thirty minutes in the segment that ends in the next stream crossing at the 2-mile mark. In a wet area (the only part of the trail that could be confusing) you stay left, then turn north to climb the hill in the steepest section so far encountered. Here even places between the switchbacks seem steeper, as you climb 400 feet in 0.5 mile in a series of a half-dozen switchbacks.

You reach an outcrop with a view of Crossett Pond. Above it the trail moderates again, still heading north, as it crosses the long shoulder of Buck. Huge white birch dot the shoulder where a small moist depression is filled with wild iris, clintonia, and polygala.

As you climb beyond the wet area, you emerge on open rock and finally see the summit. Yellow arrows on the rock point the way, but you still have 200 feet to climb. Scrub maple, birch, popple, and wild cherry fill niches near the summit, then down into a small cleft where a sign points to Shelving Rock Road, 2.5 miles away. (This yellow route is described in section 12.) Note the cleft is filled with garnet sand. You will meet garnets at about the 2400-foot level on many of the mountains in the eastern Adirondacks.

Lake George's mountains are best enjoyed in spring when the spectacle of spring flowers is at its height. Spring comes early to these foothills of the Adirondacks, so an early May walk is best. You will find the return trip takes only an hour and twenty minutes, but that the four hour estimate for the round trip does not allow for enjoying the spectacle of the panorama from the summit.

5 Butternut Brook and Pilot Knob
Paths

Pilot Knob overlooks the very southeastern corner of Lake George. Its summit is privately owned and wooded, but a 1900-foot knob on its northwestern flanks offers lovely views of the lake. Two paths lead to the knob and both share the same beginning as the western trail to Buck Mountain, section 4. The western approach is very steep; the eastern is a much gentler climb, but longer. The two routes can be combined to make an interesting loop.

Follow the Buck Mountain Trail for five minutes, about 0.3 mile, to the second intersection where you turn right away from the Buck Mountain Trail. The route is unmarked, except informally by plastic ribbons, but it is well-used and generally follows the south bank of Butternut Brook. Walk along it for about ten minutes; less than 1 mile from the start, you enter a growth of young hemlocks. A cairn with yellow paint is on the right, just beside the trail. A narrow path on the right leads to a crossing of a small brook and (within view of the cairn) begins to ascend Pilot Knob in a southerly direction.

The faint path south is marked with can lids and pieces of plastic tape. It climbs continuously, and quite steeply in places, angling to a more southeasterly course 1.6 miles from the start. You reach two open ledges before the 1900-foot knob at 2.1 miles, where there are views stretching from French Mountain to the Tongue Mountain range.

Since two hours is more than ample for the climb, you may want to vary the return. If you descend to Butternut Brook and turn left, the way you came, your return trip takes a little over an hour. If you turn right at that intersection, you can continue to follow the Butternut Brook Valley southeast. In less than ten minutes, 0.5 mile, the path leads you beside a noisy, rocky waterfall. It then rises to stay high above the brook with its lovely cascades. You may find the path somewhat overgrown. Fifteen minutes from the waterfall, at 1.7 miles from the parking area on the Butternut Brook path, 3.9 miles if you also climb Pilot Knob, the path intersects the trail from Sly Pond Road, section 7. At the intersection, head northwest, descending sharply to cross Butternut Brook, then ascending slightly for 100 yards to an intersection at 4.1 miles. Here the way right, north, is the upper part of the Buck Mountain Trail and the way left is the lower part of that trail, which heads downhill, northwest. Taking the left fork, it is nearly a twenty minute walk to the Butternut Brook crossing. In another five minutes, you reach the point you turned from the Buck Mountain Trail to walk along Butternut Brook and five minutes later your car at 5.6 miles.

A third variation requires walking directly east from the trailhead to the fork to Butternut Brook, then southeast along the brook as above. When you reach the intersection, at 1.7 miles, with the trail from Sly Pond Road, section 7, continue southeast along it for nearly fifteen minutes, about 0.7 mile. Here a fairly obvious footpath forks right, southwest. It is sporadically marked with yellow tapes and climbs southwest through a draw formed by a small stream for 0.8 mile to a saddle between the 1900-foot knob and the summit. You can turn southeast toward the summit for some views from the grassy patches or pause to pick blueberries. A right turn, northwest, leads 0.3 mile across the knob with views. Here you will easily pick up the path from Butternut Brook. This climb with a descent via the trail on the northwestern slopes completes a counterclockwise loop of 5.6 miles. It may be the easiest and best way to enjoy Pilot Knob.

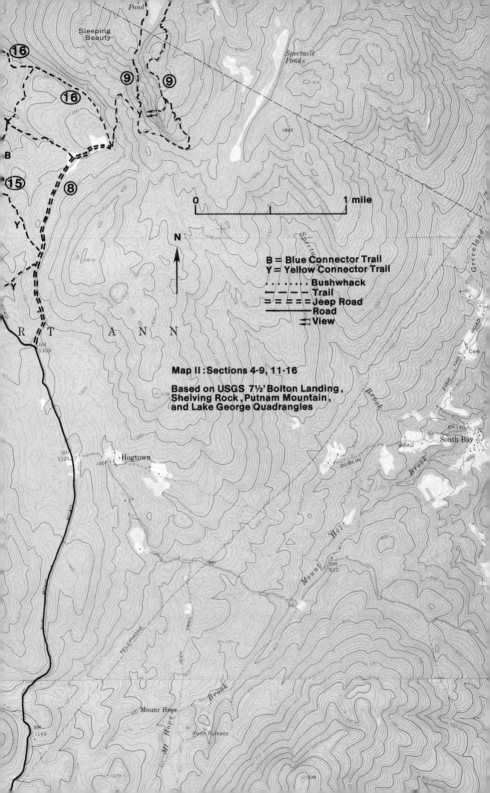

Pond

Sleeping
Beauty

Spectacle
Ponds

16

16

9

9

B

15

8

Y

Y

0   1/mile

N

B = Blue Connector Trail
Y = Yellow Connector Trail
∙∙∙∙∙∙∙ Bushwhack
— — — — Trail
= = = = = Jeep Road
———— Road
View

Map II: Sections 4-9, 11-16

Based on USGS 7½' Bolton Landing,
Shelving Rock, Putnam Mountain,
and Lake George Quadrangles

R T   A N N

BM
1309

BM
1328

Hogtown

Cem

South Bay

BM 140

DUBLIN

ROAD

Brook

Mount Hope

BM
510

TELEPHONE

JEEP TRAIL

Mount Hope

Zion Furnace

Brook

BM
1149

6 Inman Pond

Horse trail and snowmobile trail, hiking, camping, cross-country skiing
2.5 mile loop, 1½ hour, 300-foot elevation change

The trail to Inman Pond begins from a large trailhead in an area known as Hogtown. To reach the trailhead, go east 6 miles east of NY 9 on NY 149 and turn north on Buttermilk Falls Road. You will probably not be aware of the place where Buttermilk Falls Road changes its name to Sly Pond Road. The macadam ends at 3.4 miles, and at 6.5 miles you reach a large parking area and the trailhead.

The trail is an old logging road, beginning just south of the parking lot. It is flat at first, then ascends slightly to continue level to an intersection at 0.5 mile, a ten minute walk. The way straight ahead, across a new bridge over a small stream, is the continuation of the blue horse trail. A sharp right with no noted destination is the route to Inman Pond. It has red horse trail markers as well as snowmobile markers.

The trail is to the right of the small stream and ascends moderately for 0.3 mile, then levels off, swings left, and climbs moderately with another stream below on the right. It levels again and reaches another intersection at 1 mile, a quarter hour from the first intersection. Here the red-marked horse trail goes right while a yellow-marked horse trail (also bearing snowmobile disks) heads left.

If you stay on the red trail, the right fork, you cross an outlet of Inman Pond and can see the shallow pond and an old beaver dam to your left. The logging road is wide and level and skirts the pond whose shores are lined with hemlock. There is a steep bank up to the right. The pond, which is filling in, is dotted with tiny islands of leatherleaf, some of which have small pines growing on them. About seven minutes from the red-yellow fork, the trail turns left off the logging road and drops down to the shore of the pond. Bafflingly, there is about 100 feet of open water and across on the opposite shore are two snowmobile markers. Obviously, after the ice has thickened skiers as well as snowmobilers can continue, but what of the hiker and horseman? Before you turn around, notice that to the right there is a deeper portion of the pond, without the boggy islands and there are interesting rocky cliffs near the end of the pond.

If you return to the red-yellow intersection and take the yellow left fork, follow it past the end of the pond. It crosses another outlet and, lined by hemlock on both sides, leaves the shore of the pond. It drops slightly, then crosses a wet area, and again parallels the shore of the pond. After a five minute walk, the trail turns to the right away from the logging road, crosses the wet area again, winds through the woods and reaches the shore opposite the end of the red trail. Both sides of the pond have been used for camping.

When Inman Pond is frozen, it obviously makes a very good ski loop and the only part that would be challenging for the novice would be the return to the first junction, but the trip in should give you an idea of what to expect here.

7 Hogtown to Buck Mountain or Pilot Knob
Part snowmobile trail, hiking, expert cross-country skiing
4.2 miles, 2¼ hour, 1000-foot elevation change

The red trail used for the first 0.5 mile of the trek to Inman Pond continues west to intersect the Buck Mountain Trail. This route makes a good alternate for the climb up the mountain as well as a hiking or expert ski route through to Pilot Knob, 4.6 miles from Hogtown.

From the first intersection described in section 6, take the blue trail across the bridge. You begin to ascend moderately with occasional level stretches. You need to keep your eye on the trail markers since now and then another log road will fork off from the trail. At about 1 mile, the trail levels and after some gentle up and down, crosses a brook then passes through a pretty, shallow valley. The first 1.6 miles is reasonable novice to intermediate skiing, but after this shallow valley, you begin a series of steep, rather rocky descents, separated by level stretches. As you descend, so does Butternut Brook, with some nice tumbles, but no distinct waterfalls. From at least one place, you can spot the blue waters of Lake George through the trees. There are some nice rocky cliffs to the right, while the steep sides of Pilot Knob are to your left. It is the 1-mile, steep descent before you cross Butternut Brook that gives this through trip an expert ski rating.

At 2.6 miles you reach a level stretch. The overgrown path along Butternut Brook, section 5, is straight ahead. This less traveled route leading to Pilot Knob along the south side of Butternut Brook is especially nice. The way to the right, northwest, is the last of the sharp descents and leads to a crossing of Butternut Brook. Beyond the crossing, there is a gentle ascent for 100 yards to the intersection with the Buck Mountain trail, section 4. It will lead you north to the mountain or west to Pilot Knob.

behind the hotel not yet recovered, but Knapp never harvested any more timber on his land. He continued to acquire property on the eastern shore until he had nearly eight miles of shoreline and 7625 acres.

Knapp built a fabulous frame house for himself on the slopes of Shelving Rock and a private railway to bring family and guests from the dock. Eventually, he had the hotel dismantled. His home burned in 1917.

Today all but a small part of the original estate is public land. The eighty miles of carriage roads and trails built for the hotel and the estate, some following the older routes of logging roads, are now the basis of the area's trail system. Trails zigzag up mountains, making gentle switchbacks, leading to Erebus, Sleeping Beauty, and Black Mountain, as well as to Shelving Rock. They have been designated as horse, snowmobile, and hiking trails. On these, the hiker will find a variety of destinations, waterfalls, vistas, ponds, and deep woods, all on well-designed routes through mature forests. The tall maples, beech, and birch are among our forest's most notable, and the stands of hemlock and pine are as they must have been when white man first saw them. The walking trails through the pines and hemlocks are whispering routes, the whispering of the wind through high needled branches, the whispering of footsteps made quiet on needle covered trails, and the whispering of hikers responding in awe to the depth of the forest.

There is quite a bit of overlap in the designation of the seventy miles of modern trails which includes forty-one miles of horse trails, sixty-one miles of snowmobile trails, and forty-two miles of foot trails. Although hikers might usually find it better to avoid trails open to horsemen, this is not the case in the Shelving Rock network. Use by horsemen is sporadic and fairly limited. Even on peak days in spring and fall when horsemen gather at Dacy Clearing, there are no more than fifty of them. They usually stick to the routes along the better constructed carriage roads, where the surface is still so firm that horses' hooves make little impression.

The honeycomb of trails so densely covers Shelving Rock, Sleeping Beauty, and the slopes of Erebus that describing and walking every segment could be rather dull. Instead, I have broken the trails into a series of loops of various lengths, all suitable for day hiking, all amenable to combinations of greater lengths for longer camping and backpacking excursions, and all passing at least one point of interest. Other sets of loops originate at Black Mountain Point or at Pike Brook Trailhead, and after introducing these trailheads in later chapters, this guide deals with longer loops that could originate at any one of the trailheads. However, while some of the connector segments are omitted, they are mentioned in the text and all intersections, marked and unmarked are described, to avoid

confusion for hikers as they walk between the intersections of the generally unmarked maze.

A *word of caution is needed. As some sections indicate, the marking of trails
is often confusing. Furthermore, the state is not now maintaining some portions
of trail, particularly the yellow connectors leading to Lake George.*

To drive to the trailhead for the Shelving Rock area, take Northway
Exit 20, head north on NY 9, and then east on NY 149. Buttermilk Falls
Road heads north nearly 6 miles from the intersection of NY 9 and 149,
and becomes Sly Pond Road. Hogtown Road forks right, or east, from Sly
Pond Road, 8.7 miles north of NY 9. You can follow Hogtown Road as
it winds through abandoned farmland down the slopes to intersect County
Route 16, just south of South Bay on Lake Champlain. For those who
like to follow old dirt roads, this is as wild a road as you can find, and
its equally wild history has been published by the Washington County
Historical Society in a book by Fred Tracy Stiles, entitled *From Then Till
Now.* Near the intersection are apple trees remaining from the Crow Orchard.

Continuing north on Sly Pond Road you reach, at 9.5 miles, the main
DEC parking area for the Shelving Rock area trails. Shelving Rock Road
forks left, west. Notice that you have been climbing gradually throughout
those 9.5 miles. The trailhead at 1309 feet gives you a 1000-foot lead over
the mountain climbs begun from lake level.

8 Dacy Clearing

Hiking, skiing, horseback riding
1.6 miles, 40 minutes, relatively level

Dacy Clearing is 1.4 miles north of the main DEC trailhead over a dirt
road that is not barred to vehicular traffic. For most people the short, easy
walk to the clearing is a pleasant start toward Sleeping Beauty and points
beyond. Red markers designate the road. In 0.6 mile, two trails branch
left. The yellow trail leads 0.5 mile to Shelving Rock Road and 3 miles
to Buck Mountain summit, 6.3 miles to Shelving Rock, sections 8 and
9. A second intersection, also unmarked, less than 0.1 mile farther, is the
beginning of a 0.5-mile connector to a loop trail, section 12. This yellow
marked connector begins at a gate.

The road you are following once led to the Dacy Farm, the largest on
the Knapp Estate. The road is still edged with stone fences and rows of
unusual old maples, rotting and nearly dead, but forests have filled most

Road

Trail

Bushwhack

Jeep Road

View

Shelter

0   1 mile

N

Map III: Sections 8-11, 13-24, 26-27, 35

Based on N.Y .Dept. of Transportation
7½' Shelving Rock and Whitehall
Quadrangles

of the fields that once produced nearly 2000 bushels of potatoes, vegetables, and fruit for the hotels. It's little more than a thirty minute, 1.4 mile walk to the first clearing. Elderberries, blackberries, and raspberries border the small field that is regularly mowed. Near the huge maple to the right of the road you can poke among the bushes and find the foundations of the farm house. On the west side of the clearing, hidden near a cellar hole in the tall grass of summer, is the beginning of a 0.6 mile horse trail, also marked yellow, which follows a small brook and also connects with the carriage road of section 15.

The open field provides a spectacular view of the cliffs on Sleeping Beauty, and perhaps you can discern the shape that inspired the mountain's name. Beyond the field you go down and across a bridge; the road splits just past the bridge. The right fork is newer, straighter, less eroded. Both forks bring you to the clearing and the trailhead. This clearing is edged in pine and the cliffs appear to loom directly overhead. The road curves to the right through the field, and here the trail to Sleeping Beauty enters the woods 1.6 miles from the trailhead.

You may have noted a second intersection just west of the Sleeping Beauty Trail. This route leads to two privies. The continuing trail, section 16, is suitable for horsemen and also an excellent ski trail. It provides a trek below the steep slopes of Sleeping Beauty, with two connections to the old Dacy Clearing Road and one to the Shelving Rock Brook Trail.

The accompanying map suffices as a description for the two short horse trails that branch south of the Dacy Clearing Road. None of them leads immediately to vistas and, although all provide good forest walks, in summer you will probably prefer other routes described in this chapter. Those connectors will prove useful in winter if you are planning a longer circuit walk, see section 25. Note that none of the intersections with the Dacy Clearing Road are marked, and some intersections are actually difficult to spot, especially in summer.

9 Sleeping Beauty, Bumps Pond, and Bumps Pond Overlook

Hiking, snowshoeing
4.5 mile loop from Dacy Clearing, 2½ hours, 1038-foot vertical rise

From the northeast corner of Dacy Clearing a broad, wide road heads north. It is now marked as a trail, but its base was clearly well built up by boulders, making it suitable for carriages. The surface, however, is eroded. The roadway or trail leads up slopes covered with tall, straight maples, and arrives in only fifteen minutes at an intersection 0.6 mile from Dacy Clearing and over 300 feet above it. The sign says the ascent of Sleeping Beauty Summit is 1049 feet from the intersection, a vertical rise more appropriate for the clearing below. Such signs make you have little faith in the distances proclaimed.

The guideboards also state that it is 1.3 miles to the left on a red trail, (also marked for horses) to Bumps Pond, 2.1 miles from Fishbrook Pond, and 1.2 miles on the yellow trail to the right to Sleeping Beauty. It is really 1.9 miles to Fishbrook Pond from the intersection.

In order to make the loop over Sleeping Beauty's summit in a counterclockwise direction, head right, doubling back almost south below the ledges through a swampy area that can be a problem in spring. Logs placed in the muck are barely sufficient to keep you dry. The trail turns east and continues east or a little south of east below the ledges, rising slightly. At 1.1 miles the trail makes a sharp hairpin turn to the north to begin the ascent. The trail, now a narrow footpath, is still carefully built up with rock so it can traverse right across the face of the lower cliff edges. A series of switchbacks aids the climb. The cover becomes more sparse with lady's slippers capping the open patches. You reach an unmarked intersection, on a ridge at 1.7 miles. The 700-foot, just over a mile, climb between intersections is so easily accomplished on the well-designed trail that you will probably need no more than forty minutes for that segment. At the intersection head left 150 yards to the top of the cliffs. You will return to take the right fork and continue north to Bumps Pond and the rest of the circuit.

The overlook atop the cliffs offers a wide vista. The mountains of Vermont rise beyond the outline of the Champlain Valley to the east. The long valley north of Fort Ann is seen beyond the sleeping one's beautiful rock profile. The long ridge headed southeast leads from Little Buck to Buck Mountain to the waters of Lake George. To the west the mountain falls quickly away to the back of Shelving Rock. Green Island is clearly distinguishable over Shelving Rock Bay, with the cliffs on Cat Mountain across Lake George behind the island. Further left, over open water, the skyline is marked with Crane Mountain, Mt. Blue, Moose and Baldhead mountains. Continuing in a counterclockwise direction Hadley is seen as part of the long ridge beyond. North of Crane, the Blue Hills and Black and Eleventh mountains lead in a clockwise direction to Gore Mountain, with Puffer, Moxham, Santanoni, and finally Marcy in the High Peaks. Hoffman Mountain is viewed over the shoulder of Erebus. First Peak is

seen beyond that shoulder that cuts off all but the top of French Point Mountain.

Best of all is the view straight down to Dacy Clearing and the ledges and cliffs themselves.

You return to the intersection and a fork north now takes you on a walk along the ridge that makes up the summit of Sleeping Beauty. The route is up and down through boggy summit areas and across ferny glens of birch, spruce, hemlock, and pine. You wind below the summit proper, down and level, then down through a series of short, heavily wooded switchbacks, and across the ledges above Bumps Pond before finally dropping down to the outlet stream. Here at 2.5 miles you are greeted by a beaver dam and lovely little ledges at the outlet.

Across the stream, an intersection is marked by a guideboard. Your descent to it should have taken less than thirty minutes. Signs point north to the yellow trail, section 10, and state it is 1.5 miles to Fishbrook Lean-to—the distance is to the northern lean-to, around the shore. The closer southern one is less than a mile away. This trail also connects with Black Mountain Point, 7.2 miles away, and Pike Brook Road, 6.4 miles away, sections 19 and 23. Since beaver are no longer so active at Bumps Pond, its pretty shoreline has returned, but it is pretty shallow for swimming. You may prefer to walk north to the Fishbrook Pond for a swim before returning.

Heading south along the western shore of Bumps Pond, the red trail follows an old road bed. At 2.6 miles the roadway is flooded in the area around an intersection with a yellow marked horse trail. The sign says to Erebus Mountain, and that ambiguously implies a summit. The trail really heads 0.6 mile northwest toward a wooded intersection on Erebus, section 21, passing a good spring just 200 yards from Bumps Pond.

If you look closely, just before, north of, the Erebus Intersection you will spot a second yellow marked trail heading away from the lake. No guideboard points to its destination, designated Bumps Pond Overlook. The path that leads straight uphill is not well marked; and, unfortunately, new growth obscures the lovely view so that you can only enjoy it when the leaves are off.

Return to the red trail and continue south. At 3 miles near the southern end of Bumps Pond the trail enters a field with a gorgeous old stone chimney. A hunting lodge once stood here as part of the Knapp estate, a destination served by the estate's carriage roads. The clearing around the lodge site is the only good camping place on Bumps Pond.

You continue on the roadway, south, climbing into a saddle bordered by ledges. The ones on the left are the base of the cliffs of Sleeping Beauty. Five minutes walking from the height-of-land through the narrow gorge, look for a little natural chimney standing in the woods, a shard fallen from the cliffs. Continue down to an overlook through a narrow cut with a pretty but small vista south. Crane and Buck mountains are a part of it. The road becomes wider and rockier, zigzagging along the well built rock base that was beautifully constructed to hug the hillside. Several small overlooks are passed; each could provide a taste of what is to come if you had chosen to make the circuit in a clockwise direction.

The steep pitches end at 3.9 miles at the intersection 0.6 mile from Dacy Clearing. Here you are 2.2 miles from Shelving Rock Road, not 3.1 as the sign indicates.

10 Fishbrook Pond from Bumps Pond
Hiking, camping, fishing
0.8 mile, 20 minutes, 200-foot descent

From the intersection at the north end of Bumps Pond, a spot made pretty by ledges through which the outlet is carved, a roadway heads north beside the outlet. The route is marked with yellow disks. It is the link in a complicated chain that makes several round-trip loops possible. These range from the Erebus Loop, section 21, to the tremendous backpacking trip from Shelving Rock Trailhead to Dacy Clearing over Sleeping Beauty, past Bumps, Fishbrook, Millman, and Black Mountain ponds, to Black Mountain Point, and back along the shore to Shelving Rock and up to the trailhead. As later sections show, the honeycomb of trails is so intricate that at least a half dozen other loops passing Bumps Pond can be devised, and most will use this segment.

The roadway follows the outlet, which is at present flooded by new beaver work, then continues a little east of north as the outlet of Bumps Pond heads east. The grade is so slight that the route is apt to have water problems, and in rainy times, the half-log bridges are not always sufficient to provide dry footing. The roadway was constructed along a remarkably straight course, hardly veering at all as it descends through a long draw to the southwest corner of Fishbrook Pond. Directly ahead, a path leads to a camping promontory on the shore. A marked trail east leads to a second lean-to on the southern shore 200 yards away. The trail continues around the eastern shore to the intersection, section 27.

11 Shelving Rock Road

Hiking, horseback riding, skiing
3.5 miles, 1¼ hours, 900-foot descent

Two routes first brought visitors to Shelving Rock. One was by water. Lumbermen came by boat to cut the massive pines and float them in rafts to the foot of the lake for portage to Ticonderoga. Other softwoods were harvested for building materials, and the hardwoods were cut to make charcoal for iron furnaces. Each furnace at the ironworks north along Lake Champlain consumed, in one day, a timbered acre of charcoal.

Lake George's thirty-two mile length was an ideal waterway, for wars or transportation. The second commercially operated steamboat in the world was put in service on its waters in 1809. Steamers plied the lake until the 1930s, bringing guests to the Hundred Island House, built at Shelving Rock in 1875, and to the Pearl Point House, built in 1876. For nearly two decades they accommodated guests in the elegant wilderness style of the period—rowboat trips, excursions on the lake, dances, walks, or carriage rides to nearby hills.

The second route to Shelving Rock, over land, began near Fort Ann. It first served settlers who logged the hills or mined iron ore near Mount Hope. It also served the farmers who turned their hogs out in summer into the forests of beech, butternut, chestnut, and oak to fatten them on acorns and nuts. Their settlement became known as Hogtown. The "over the mountain" road went through Hogtown, down the mountains to Shelving Rock, permitting farmers to sell milk and potatoes and fresh vegetables to the hotels on the lake shore.

Shelving Rock Road drops almost 1000 feet in the 3.5 miles between the main DEC parking area and the edge of private land on the old Knapp Estate. The road is narrow, almost entirely one lane. There are few adequate parking spots along it, even adjacent to major trails. The trail intersections are so close together along the road you can usually count on parking near the one you want, but it could happen that you might have to walk along the road to reach the trail you choose.

The road is improved with macadam on the steeper grades. Nevertheless, spring washouts often severely erode the surface, and care must be used. There are a few very steep grades. In midwinter through early spring, the road is often impassable.

The following chart gives distances to the trailheads for loops described. Many of the trailhead signs are missing, and the problems of keeping them in place defy the abilities of the local ranger.

Main DEC parking area for trailhead for Shelving Rock System	0.0
Buck Mountain—North Trail	0.5
Shelving Rock—Dacy Clearing road loop interchange	1.15
Parking turnout—stream	1.35
Shelving Rock Brook Trail—northern loop	2.5
Blue Horse Trail—Big Bridges Trail	2.6
Shelving Rock Mountain Trailhead	2.75
Lower Falls Trail	2.85
Trail to Log Bay	3.45
Private land and gate (NO parking nearby)	3.5

12 Buck Mountain from the North

Hiking, snowshoeing
2.5 miles, 1¾ hour, 1150-foot vertical rise

There is an easier way to reach the views on Buck Mountain than the climb from Pilot Knob, section 4. The trail from Shelving Rock Road takes advantage of the elevation gained by the "over the mountain" roads, and starts at 1180 feet. The trailhead for the yellow marked trail is 0.5 mile west of the principal parking area. There is room for only one or two cars near the trailhead, so you are advised to start your walk from that parking area. This adds 1 mile to the round trip, making it 6 miles and about three and a half hours.

The beginning of the trail is relatively level. You cross an intermittent stream after ten minutes, near where the stream drops into a ravine on your right. Shortly there is a small swamp on the left. You continue, winding a relatively level course through hemlock stands, to reach, after a half hour and just short of a mile, a stream flowing from left to right. Fifteen minutes later, at 1.4 miles, after a climb of over 200 feet, you reach a third stream. Crossing it, the way turns almost due west and keeps that course to the summit.

After climbing about 100 feet above the stream crossing, you pass big boulders on your right, then turn to follow the brook more closely. In another hundred feet you pass between two very large boulders.

The climbing becomes even steeper, and after 2 miles, about one and a quarter hours, you enter a small gorge. This leads you to the summit. Within ten minutes, about 0.25 mile farther, you can scramble to the first vista, an opening to the north. In the last 0.25 mile the trail angles slightly left and enters a large crevice or notch, then emerges in the cleft below the summit.

The best views are from the summit. However, only an overlook south of the trail, just before it reaches the top, has views of Vermont. From it, on a clear day, you can see Mount Mansfield, Camel's Hump, Pico, and Killington mountains. Along the open summit in mid-summer, you will find a profusion of blueberries.

13 Shelving Rock Loop

Hiking, swimming, snowmobiling
4.7-mile-loop, 4 hours, 1300-foot elevation change

At the main DEC parking area for the Shelving Rock system, turn left, west on Shelving Rock Road toward Lake George. The trailhead for the Shelving Rock Mountain Trail usually has adequate parking, so it is possible to drive the 2.75 miles to it.

Enormous pines surmount the ledges near the parking area, a foretaste of what is to come. The yellow marked trail heads northeast, following an old carriage road. Within 100 yards a barrier to vehicular traffic is reached and within three minutes, shorter than the 0.25 mile the sign indicates, you reach an intersection. The way left points to Shelving Rock summit. The sign says it is 1.5 miles distant with a 735-foot ascent. The sign is wrong; it is only a 520-foot climb. You will be even more suspicious of signs when you leave the lakeshore for a return climb. The sign there at a much lower elevation gives the same information; and from lakeshore the climb is 813 feet.

The way left, your route, has red hiking and orange snowmobile trail markers; by this time the confusion of sign colors should also begin to bother you. There are many inconsistencies in the Shelving Rock area: the use of two or more colors for a given trail is a common, but poor practice, and the designation of more than two trails by the same color, as is done at several intersections, is equally confusing.

The carriage roads on the Knapp estate were built with carefully graded stone base. Tight switchbacks make easy grades, even on steep slopes. The century since the roads were built has seen them blend into the rocky hills. Mosses and lichens cover the rocks, pine needles pave the surface. Finer walking trails do not exist in the Adirondacks. These are trails in the Eu-

Over the Mountain to the East Shore of Lake George

STATE LANDS ALONG Lake George were incorporated into the Forest Preserve for the same reasons lands elsewhere were so acquired: their valuable timbers were gone, and conservationists wished to protect the forests in the future. However, part of the land along Lake George's eastern shore was preserved in a special way, and the fruits of that preservation today make the forests of Shelving Rock among the most beautiful in the Adirondacks.

Even before the first big hotels were built on the lake's southern shore, steamers began to take passengers the length of Lake George's waters. The *Vermont* in 1809, the *James Caldwell* in 1817, the *Mountaineer* in 1824, and the 144-foot *Minne-Ha-Ha* in 1857 began the long tradition of regular passenger runs. Rough hotels that served lumbermen were converted to accommodate tourists. Because of the steamer service, hotels could be built north along the lake shore at many points otherwise almost inaccessible by land.

Among these were the Fourteen Mile Island House that opened in 1860 on the island off Shelving Rock. In 1875 the Hundred Island House was built on the point north of Log Bay, beneath Shelving Rock. Here, guests vacationed in an opulent style, elegantly dressed, with servants to care for their every need, and superbly prepared meals. The story of those lost times and the romantic era of steamboating is beautifully told in Elsa Kay Steinback's *Sweet Peas and a White Bridge*, recommended reading as the best introduction to Lake George's eastern shore.

In 1894, when fire struck the Hundred Island House, it was bought at auction by George O. Knapp, a founder of Union Carbide Corporation. His agents maintained the Hundred Island House for a time, remodeling it and modernizing it, adding gardens and a telegraph wire, and carriage roads and hiking trails with rustic open houses as resting places.

The slopes behind the hotel had been cut many years before; most lumbering in the region ceased before 1850. Photographs still show the forests

View of Sleeping Beauty from Dacy Clearing

ropean sense, civilized and graceful, a welcome change from the mud paths that usually greet Adirondack hikers.

The dry southern slopes of the mountain are covered with hardwoods, predominantly oak. Walking beneath them, you quickly attain a level with a partial view of Lake George, then drop to a small valley and a four-way trail intersection at 0.8 mile. A blue trail forks right, and a yellow horse trail heads off between it and the continuing roadway. You stay left on the roadway, now marked with yellow, and start the switchbacks again, climbing steeply, circling north around the summit of Shelving Rock. At 1.15 miles, turn right to an overlook promontory looking directly at First Peak with the deep valley separating it from French Point Mountain to the right. The islands of the Narrows are directly below you.

Retrace your steps for 100 yards, then continue along the roadway toward the summit. Shortly, you reach a rock outcrop with a view of the Sagamore complex. The summit, reached at 1.3 miles after a forty minute walk, is becoming overgrown. The open view is limited to the south and east, but you can see Fan Hill or Little Buck, Buck Mountain, and Pilot Knob Mountain peeking over Buck's shoulder. You look down the lake toward Lake George Village. In the west lie Crane, Cat, and the Tongue Mountain Range. Over the tree tops you can see the summits of Black, Erebus, and Sleeping Beauty. An unmarked path south takes you in two minutes to an overlook above Log Bay.

The entire climb so far takes less than an hour, so this loop continues by returning to the trail intersection, a walk of less than ten minutes. Here at 1.8 miles, turn left, then left again in 100 feet to find the yellow trail, marked with horse trail symbols. It is a fascinating trail, one whose old rock work tells that it was built at the time of the hotels and the estate. The route is north, then west, down to a little overlook that is off the trail. From it in summer there is only a glimpse of Mountcalm Point at the tip of the Tongue and the islands of the Narrows. The forest becomes dark and beautiful, with tall hemlock hugging the sheer mountainside. The trail zigzags north again, sometimes descending with stone steps, and finally emerging on a roadway near a big boulder. The 0.6 mile drop from the intersection is scramble enough for hikers. Horsemen who have tried it once avoid it.

At 2.4 miles you have emerged beside the stone foundations of the Knapp Estate; the beautiful mosaic patterns of its brick floors are now promontories from which to view the lake. Even here, trees are crowding the view, and nothing remains of the formal gardens that once stretched below. You head north along the roadway, watching for the yellow trail markers. You will need them to guide you on the narrow traverse that cuts to a lower road. Here at 2.5 miles the way left is posted; you turn right to continue descending to lake level where the roadway is now marked with red horse trail symbols.

You have arrived at one of the great woods roads of the world. Towering hemlock make it impossible to believe that these woods were ever cut. Lush ferns in every niche between moss covered rocks edge both sides of the way. Steep banks rise on your right, and the waters of Lake George glint through the trees on your left. You walk along it for only 0.5 mile before reaching a sign that directs you south along a red marked foot trail up the shoulder of Shelving Rock toward the carriage road. From here it says it is 1.45 miles to the summit: in reality it is 0.7 mile to the intersection, from which it is 0.5 mile to the summit. But no matter. You have walked 3 miles with just over 1.5 miles left to complete the loop, part of that a stiff climb. With this in mind, you may want to choose to walk farther north along the road to swim and picnic before returning, section 18.

When you start up, sparsely placed red markers point the way beside a deep ravine. It is a wild place of unbelievably large hemlock, sheer ledges, tumbled boulders. You climb steeply, then along a more level course on smooth rock below ledges. The woods become more open as you reach the 800 foot level. You wind across a relatively level area and at 3.5 miles meet a blue trail, section 17, coming from the east through a draw on your left. You can take it for a short detour to a surprising vista. A two minute walk off the trail to your left will bring you to an overlook to the beginning of the Narrows, Point of Tongue, and First Peak.

Return and continue west through a pretty hemlock grove on the trail toward Shelving Rock. Now the dominant marker color seems to be blue, though you will also see red and snowmobile orange markers. You make a confusing hairpin turn and arrive at 3.7 miles near the intersection of the yellow trail on which you started down the mountain to the lake. Climb up a short grade to the main carriage road and turn left along it to complete the loop walk.

14 Loop to the Falls on Shelving Rock Brook and the Shores of Log Bay

Hiking, swimming, picnicking
3.2 miles, 2 hours, 200-foot elevation change

This loop takes you south of Shelving Rock Road where no camping or fires are permitted. It is a superb nature trail with lovely views of the falls and the bays of Lake George.

Park at the trailhead for Shelving Rock Summit, section 13, and walk east, then south, along Shelving Rock Road for 0.4 mile. You cross a bridge over Shelving Rock Brook. Just beyond it, turn right onto a carriage road that heads back west beside the brook. In less than 0.3 mile it leads to the falls. On the way to them you pass a pond with lovely reflections. Its stumps and alders are home to many birds, including a resident pileated woodpecker. Below, there are the remains of a dam, which was the source of power for the Knapp estate. Downstream is the lovely waterfall, but the carriage road quickly heads southwest away from the falls.

For the best look at the falls and a visit to the foundations of the old power plant, leave the road near the head of the falls and follow the footpath that leads you on a scramble to the foot of the falls. *However, do not venture to the top of the falls or along the wet rocks beside them — there have been injuries here.* The path close to the falls and its several branches continue along the brook through the deepest part of the gorge to intersect the carriage road at the lower bridge over the brook.

An alternative route is along the road as it curves away from the brook to circle around and rejoin the brook 0.4 mile away at road level. On it you pass foundations. Note the size of the cedar on the edge of the trail beside the stone work. Either way you go, at 1 mile you arrive at a bridge near the confluence of Shelving Rock Brook and Log Bay, a handsome place to stop and rest, overhung with hemlocks that frame a view to the lake made double by reflections in the protected water.

For the best view of Shelving Rock, return south along the road for 200 yards but leave the road before it heads uphill. You will find a footpath that continues south along the shore. It follows the shoreline of Log Bay, a shallow, sandy estuary filled with sunken and smoothed logs. These have been in the water for over 130 years, dating to the time a sawmill harnessed the water of Shelving Rock Brook.

The view across the lake is to the Sagamore Complex on Green Island with Cat Mountain behind. In five minutes you reach a rock ledge from which you can see back to the face of Shelving Rock. You can walk along the shore for another fifteen minutes, about 0.4 mile, before reaching private land.

When you return, continue north of the bridge over Shelving Rock Brook, staying along the lake shore. The carriage road marked with blue hiking disks winds for more than a mile along the bays and points before reaching private land again. The road leads you to a painter's paradise of deep blue-

green bays, vistas of islands, views of Buck and Little Buck mountain, hem-lock covered shorelines, the southern end of the Tongue Mountain Range, and the funny camel's hump of High Nopit and Pole Hill across the Point of Tongue.

There are two ways to return to your car: you can continue on the trail beside the water until it turns inland and within sight of private land heads east for 100 yards to intersect the road, 0.9 mile west of your car.

A prettier route would be to retrace your steps for 0.7 mile along the handsome shoreline to a point opposite Log Bay where the roadway makes a sharp turn to the northeast away from the shore. You will meet a fork 200 yards from the shore, and if you continue straight, you will climb through open boulder fields in five minutes to the main road. Head uphill for 0.1 mile. Here a carriage road heads south for 0.25 mile. It leads directly to Shelving Rock Brook right above the falls and could be used to create a different loop except that there is no longer a bridge over Shelving Rock Brook at the head of the falls. You may want to add this detour to your loop, however, since this 0.25 mile arc, which contours south and hugs the hillside, offers lovely views of the valley, sheltered here with enor-mous pines. The parking area and the start of the loop is another 0.15 mile east of the beginning of this carriage road segment.

15 Loop along the Carriage Road to Dacy Clearing

Hiking, cross-country skiing
4.45 miles, 2 hours, 800 feet elevation change

A deep woods walk without vistas begins from the parking area for Shelv-ing Rock. An alternate starting point for the loop is the main DEC park-ing area for the Shelving Rock Trail System. This would be the best beginning when Shelving Rock Road is closed to vehicles. Like all the loops in this system, the honeycomb of connector trails permits several ways to shorten or lengthen the desired loop.

Starting at the parking area for Shelving Rock, head north 0.2 mile to the trail intersection and take the right fork along the red marked trail toward Dacy Clearing 2.3 miles away. You are on the road that carried produce from the Dacy Farm to hotels near Shelving Rock. The entire route is broad and open, well enough packed that horses' hoofs do not

Shelving Rock Brook Falls

chew up the surface and fun enough for ski touring, if you can handle the 800 foot plunge, the steepest segment of which drops 200 feet in 0.2 mile.

The road follows the valley of an unnamed brook, climbing gently. You can occasionally see the water pipes that once brought water to the Knapp estate from a spring way up in a valley on the shoulder of Erebus. The description tall and straight never had more meaning than when applied to the trees along your route.

After a ten minute walk, about 0.6 mile, you cross a stream and reach a trail intersection. The sign says 2 miles to Dacy Clearing to the right. The middle route has red markings, but no hint of its destination; it is described in section 14. An enigmatic sign points to the left, 0.7 mile to Erebus and 1.7 miles to Shelving Rock summit. This yellow route is also described in section 17.

The route on the right will take you toward Dacy Clearing and it is also marked with yellow disks. You are again walking in the rich hemlock forest that shrouds the deeper valleys. You cross a second bridge in about six minutes, at 0.8 mile. Beyond it, a blue trail forks to the left to connect with the Shelving Rock Brook Trail, section 16, or with the horse trail to Dacy Clearing.

Just before a third bridge, 0.1 mile farther, a blue trail forks right. This very handsome segment takes you 0.9 mile over the Big Bridges Trail to Shelving Rock Road, section 16. It is a toss-up whether it is prettier to return this way or continue for a longer loop.

For the longer loop stay on the yellow trail, passing a gorge on your left. Big birches brighten the mixed hardwood forest, and shortly you cross another bridge. You follow the trail along the gorge, climbing steadily until the trail begins to level off at 1.4 miles and a good forty minute walk. Notice the huge basswood along the level stretch.

A four-way intersection is reached 0.3 mile farther at 1.7 miles. The yellow trail leads straight 0.6 mile to Dacy Clearing and the completion of the old farm road. To the far left there is a small blue marked trail heading into the gorge, leading in 0.4 mile to the Dacy Clearing horse trail, section 13. Note that if you choose Dacy Clearing as the beginning of the loop, the yellow trail starts at the southern of the two clearings near the cellar hole.

To complete the loop along a new set of trails, head right along a blue trail. It winds within 0.5 mile to a second four-way intersection. This one, at 2.2 miles, is, like its predecessors, without trail signs. Both routes it intersects are marked with yellow; the one on the left heads 0.5 mile back, southeast, to the Dacy Clearing road, 0.6 mile north of the main trailhead. Its intersection with that road is marked by a fence gate.

If you are following the woods walk, turn right at the four-way intersection. Towering birch line the trail as it begins to drop, at first gently, then through a series of hairpin turns. A small glimpse of Little Buck Mountain through the trees makes it seem as if an autumn walk might be best. The roadway that the trail follows is like others on the old estate; it is built up with stones to hold the base against the steep valley.

In no time at all (it is such a smooth, easy grade), you see a small pond through the trees below. You reach the road in less than ten minutes from the last intersection, a distance of 0.6 mile. In fact the entire 2.8 mile walk so far probably requires only an hour and a quarter.

Follow Shelving Rock Road to the northeast now, past the remains of an old man-made pond. Let your ears be your guide, for in about twelve minutes, at 3.3 miles, you will hear the sound of a waterfall on the small brook that accompanies the road. Turn off to explore its thirty-foot drop. Several cascades combine to make the falls and its series of small kettles worn on intervening ledges.

An easy 1.35 mile walk of twenty minutes along the road will bring you to a bridge over Shelving Rock Brook, and another 0.3 mile brings you back to your car.

16 Dacy Clearing to Log Bay

Hiking, skiing
4.1 miles, 2 hours, 1000-foot elevation change

The honeycomb of trails between Dacy Clearing and Log Bay is nowhere more evident than along this walk. A chain of loops or cells that create longer and longer circuits stretches between the two points. Taking the northernmost segment of two loops, you can create a wonderful walk west from Dacy Clearing. This walk is especially desirable when Shelving Rock Road is unsuitable for driving or at any time when you want one of the deepest and quietest woods walks possible. You can use it as an alternate return loop to the walk along the road described in section 15.

This trip can also take you west on a horse trail, past Shelving Rock Brook Falls, to the shores of Log Bay, section 14. One course for this circuit is described, but the cellular trail plan allows you to shorten the circuit at many points.

If you park at the main DEC parking area and walk to Dacy Clearing, the shortest circuit walk including this trail is 8.85 miles long. This would mean returning via Shelving Rock Road; all other circuits are longer.

At Dacy Clearing head to the northern field and spot the beginning of a blue horse trail, 100 yards to the west of the start of the trail to Bumps Pond. A trailhead sign indicates Shelving Rock Road 3.1 miles away. The first part of the horse trail follows an old log road that once climbed Sleeping Beauty, hugging the steep southwestern base. The modern horse trail continues northwest. You pass cliffs on your right at 0.5 mile as the trail continues on a long and gentle downhill. You pass a pretty brook filled with big boulders, then follow the valley of an intermittent stream that flows just below the Beauty's steepest slopes. The trail takes a wiggly course, crossing the intermittent brook several times and arriving at an intersection after an easy 1 mile walk. Here a blue trail forks left to the Dacy Clearing yellow trail, section 15. With a walk on the yellow trail, this connector completes one of the smallest cells in the honeycomb and can be used to return to Dacy Clearing. With it you have a nice ski loop for novice-to-intermediate skiers.

For the Log Bay walk, continue northwest from the intersection, a right turn on a yellow horse trail. The beginning of this section is almost too steep for cross-country skiers. Beyond a brook crossing, the trail makes another series of arcs and wiggles as it contours at a lower grade in a gentler descent. At 1.6 miles the descent quickens, and at 1.8 miles an intersection is reached.

The way right is a blue marked 0.2 mile connector to the red Shelving Rock Brook Valley Trail, section 17. This short segment makes a sharp descent to the brook, fords it, then climbs through a beautiful hemlock gorge for a little more than 100 yards to the red trail.

Your loop takes you left at the intersection, on a trail also marked with blue, for a lovely 0.5 mile segment along Shelving Rock Brook. At 2.3 miles you intersect the yellow Dacy Clearing Trail.

Take a left, uphill, on it for 0.1 mile to yet another intersection with a blue horse trail. You will leave the yellow Dacy Clearing Trail at 2.4 miles, turning right onto the blue trail which is known as the Big Bridges Trail. This 0.9 mile connector from the yellow trail to Shelving Rock Road is also designated as a snowmobile trail. It is a great ski route, but best skied at midweek when there are few snowmobiles.

The Big Bridges Trail is an aisle through a cathedral of evergreens. It follows a very scenic course along a pretty, old carriage road, which now has three huge new bridges built for horsemen. Shortly beyond the intersection, at 2.5 miles, the trail crosses a tributary of Shelving Rock Brook on the largest of these bridges, a 20-foot span supported by tremendous log and rock piers. Across the bridge, the trail turns to follow Shelving Rock Brook as it flows for several hundred feet through a gorgeous, high, rock-walled ravine secluded in deep hemlocks. A prettier woods trail does not exist.

Two smaller bridges follow, the second at 2.9 miles crossing Shelving Rock Brook. Beyond the last bridge, the trail winds across a rather level area and intersects Shelving Rock Road at 3.3 miles. Here turn left, east, down a short grade for 0.1 mile to return to Shelving Rock Brook. Turn right again onto the carriage road, section 11, for the 0.3 mile walk to the falls and continue straight on that carriage road to complete the 4.1 mile walk to the shores of Log Bay.

17 Shelving Rock Brook to Erebus Intersection, returning via the Vistas Loop

Hiking
5.6 miles, 2½ hours, 900 feet elevation change

Again head up the trail to Shelving Rock to the first intersection, 0.2 mile, section 11. Turn east, right, toward Dacy Clearing on a red horse trail that is also marked for snowmobiles, and follow it for a ten minute walk, about 0.4 mile to a second intersection. Continue straight on the red trail; its destination is unmarked. Notice the yellow trail, marked Erebus 0.7 mile, Shelving Rock 1.7 miles, coming in from the left. It is one of the two options for your return. The way right is also yellow and marked 2 miles to Dacy Clearing, section 15.

The red trail follows an old carriage road, a rather more park-like route than usual for the Adirondacks. You will walk along it as it climbs gently through alternating patches of deep hemlock and hardwoods, here huge yellow birch and dying beech. It takes about twenty minutes to cover the 0.7 mile from the last intersection to the trail's first approach to Shelving Rock Brook. You cannot help but enjoy a summer's walk along the rock-lined gorge that frames the brook sparkling with spring freshets, deep and cool beneath the hemlock. The trail becomes steeper, and the falls and cascades in the brook more numerous. There is a minor split on the way, with the snowmobile trail taking a left fork and an unmarked footpath staying closer to the stream. It is prettier walking on the stream path. The routes become one again and, shortly after, you reach an intersection. Here, after a one-hour, most pleasant woods walk, a sign points to a blue trail left, north, to Shelving Rock Summit, 2.9 miles. You have covered exactly 2 miles to reach the intersection.

You can stay on the Shelving Rock Brook Trail to continue to Bumps

Pond. Even if you do not follow this route all the way, you might wish to continue on this red trail up the valley for a bit longer. It is a truly handsome walking route that follows the brook in a valley behind the long curved shoulder of Erebus.

If you do continue northeast along it, you first cross the brook, then continue to a very long, 30-foot snowmobile bridge at about 1400-foot elevation. The small waterfalls continue throughout the gorge and the climb continues fairly steeply. The red trail reaches an intersection in another mile and 700 feet more of climbing. It is thirty minutes between intersections. At the intersection you can turn right on the yellow trail, section 21, for the 0.6 mile walk to Bumps Pond.

To complete the Vistas Loop, return to the intersection with the red and blue trail beside Shelving Rock Brook. It is marked with a sign pointing to Shelving Rock Summit. You will be heading north on the blue trail at 2 miles plus whatever distance you detoured up the valley.

The narrow blue trail first climbs into a draw, up to the top of a ridge, and into a narrower draw headed straight toward higher ground. Here at 2.4 miles, you walk straight toward the hillside, then turn sharply left in a not well marked location, around the little nose of high ground, then up and over it. Ledges cover the top, and the trail arcs around, then turns to head southwest through open forests of oak and ironwood and stunted pine. Without leaves, this is a lovely ridge for views. (You pass a concealed right fork for one of the yellow trails of section 20, but you probably will not spot it.)

As you cross over the nose you start down, traverse the south side of the hill, and complete a sharp hairpin turn to the northwest. As you return southwest from the hairpin, you reach an intersection at 2.9 miles. A yellow trail heads right, north, from the intersection, where a sign indicates the distance to lake shore is 0.8 mile. It, together with a short section of the blue trail you have just completed, is a segment of section 20.

The blue trail is now quite obviously following one of the old carriage roads, but it shows little signs of any use in recent years. You round a small knob and cross a draw that falls off steeply on your left, walking just below the summit of the ridge on your right. Again you cross over the brow of the ridge; the lake is visible through the trees on your right. You parallel the spine of the ridge, making an arc around one of the knobs along it. You cross one steep ravine that falls off to Shelving Rock Brook Valley. Buck Mountain is visible through the trees. The trail hugs the right side of the ravine and then emerges at the first vantage at 3.6 miles. The walk

Big Bridges Trail

following the blue trail across the ridges from the red Shelving Rock Brook trail to the vantages takes just over half an hour.

You look down on another in the chain of small hills that form the shoulder of Erebus. That hill lies between you and Shelving Rock. Your view is directly across Shelving Rock Brook Valley to Buck and Little Buck mountains. The steepness of the valley is sharply delineated from this vantage. But the best part of the vista is the sideways view of the cliffs on Sleeping Beauty.

Continuing on the blue trail, you head sharply away from the valley, following a level contour on the side of a steep draw. A traverse, followed by a hairpin turn on the sharp hillside, takes you at 3.8 miles to an intersection with a yellow trail that forks left, south.

You can follow the yellow trail to complete a loop. You will find it plunges directly down into the draw along a narrow rocky course. The top of the dry valley is filled with ferns, including maidenhair. It is a wild, steep-sided place, shadowed by tall maples. It only takes a few minutes to drop to more level terrain, back in hemlock forests. Watch for the giant basswood, a rarity in the mountains now. The trail levels out and curves around a small swamp, then descends again, and within fifteen minutes you have made the 0.7 mile descent on the yellow trail, intersecting the red trail. Here, at 4.5 miles, you turn right along the red trail for the return to your car. The total time for this 5.1 mile loop is less than two and a half hours.

A 0.5 mile longer and preferable loop, with an additional vista, can be made by continuing along the blue trail on the ridge. Beyond the intersection with the yellow trail, the blue trail is relatively level, dropping down only to a small swamp and skirting it on the left. Within twenty minutes you cross the 0.7 mile of level hilltop to discover a great vista looking south. The view from this vantage, which is off the trail to the right, is said to surpass that from Shelving Rock.

Beyond that overlook, you cross a draw and in a matter of only a couple minutes intersect the red trail from the lake, section 13. Here at 4.6 miles, you turn left, following the blue and red marked trail until it zigzags confusingly into a hollow, then climbs to the main road up Shelving Rock at 4.8 miles. Again turn left to follow the carriage road trail back to the trailhead.

Return from the second vista should be under half an hour. The entire 5.6 mile circuit requires less than three hours.

Lake George—
Islands and Shores

LAKE GEORGE'S 200 or so islands vary from Long Island's 1.2 mile span to unnamed rocks whose dimensions are measured in feet. Their number does not approach the nineteenth century guidebook writer's claim of an island for each day of the year, but their beauty certainly exceeds even the wildest descriptions.

From Dome Island with its regular evergreen cap to Sarah and Hazel that shelter the deep green waters of Paradise Bay, from the Mother Bunch to Scotch Bonnet, the islands present an array of beauty and intriguing nomenclature that has fascinated visitors for years.

Only a handful are privately owned. The rest, managed by DEC along with the eastern shoreline, offer a variety of campsites, moorings, picnic, and day use areas for every type of boater.

Campers along the shore, those arriving via trails from Shelving Rock or Black Mountain, should note that they are under the same restrictions as visitors who arrive by water. Camping permits are required for the shoreline campsites, and may be obtained by visiting the Island headquarters at Glen Island, or by calling a toll-free reservation number. Campsites are numbered and assigned, and a fee is charged from Memorial Day to September 15. At other times camping is free. Two lean-tos, at Commission Point and Black Mountain Point, are for shelter only; no camping is permitted at them.

Several good maps that locate and name the islands are available. The best is the DEC folder, "The Islands of Lake George."

The preservation of the state's island bounty can be traced to the work of one man, John S. Apperson. From the early 1900s until his death in 1963, he single-handedly led the movement to save the islands, and his work as a conservation leader was a model and an inspiration for many in New York State who continue the work that ensures the protection of the Forest Preserve. Apperson toted tons of rip-rap to build up the eroding island shoreline, combatting both high water and the damaging waves of steamboats. He led the fight to keep the Tongue Mountain Highway from the route along the Narrows. He was a leader in the legal fight to prove that the state, not the federal government, had the right to control the lake's water level. Those who knew him were most impressed by his audacity in threatening some of the 900 squatters who had established illegal residency on the precious islands. The fact that most of the squatters were evicted by a court of law through his expert evidence is not nearly as exciting as his threats to burn out illegal occupants if they did not choose to move in a timely manner. The fight was won, and today the islands are there for all.

Several trails on the east shore of Lake George are accessible by water, from docks managed by the DEC. Every trail in this chapter has an alternate trailhead, accessible by land, but the climbs from water level are challenging and special.

18 The Eastern Shore, Black Mountain Point to Shelving Rock

3.6 miles, 2 hours, minimal elevation change

There may not be a more pleasant level walk in the world than this one. Every step you take along the 4.6 miles of Lake George's eastern shoreline offers something of beauty: the changing outlooks of islands, peninsulas, and rock ledges momentarily trapped in the frame of overhanging boughs, and the transition from deep, dark woods to vistas of sky and water rimmed with steep mountains.

Black Mountain Point is a day use area with dock facilities, picnic tables, rest rooms, and a lean-to for shelter, not for camping. The northeast side of the point encloses a small harbor. On your first visit, you cannot help but see the large iron ring firmly affixed to a rock on the point. That ring once moored the steamer *Minne-Ha-Ha* when she served as a floating hotel and restaurant during the 1870s and 1880s. Cyrus Butler, whose iron company, the Horicon Works of Lake Champlain, had harvested most of the hardwoods on Lake George's eastern shore for charcoal, used the steamer as the nucleus of a resort on the point. His "Horicon Pavilion," built above Black Mountain Point, was a monumental log cabin, the porches of which were decorated with elaborate ornamentation and delicate tracery of wooden branches woven in open geometric patterns.

As you start to walk south of Black Mountain Point, the views are of French Point and its namesake mountain. At 0.4 mile you see a trail branching east up the mountain, section 21. Beyond the junction the main trail, infrequently marked with red disks, ducks back from the shoreline for 0.5 mile, where at 0.9 mile, a second trail, also unmarked heads up the mountain, section 20. Beyond this junction, the red trail stays completely out of sight of the shoreline as it passes two peninsulas, the second of which forms the northern enclosing arm of Paradise Bay. Red Rock Peninsula is the southern arm, but to see those red rocks, walk along that point's southern shore, the shore that edges Red Rock Bay.

The trail forks at 1.6 miles, the way west leads past Paradise Bay to the peninsula, then goes back to rejoin the eastern route at 1.9 miles, near Red Rock Bay.

As you leave Red Rock Bay, look for a yellow marked horse trail at 2 miles. This trail up the mountainside is the end of the trip described in section 20.

South of Red Rock Bay, the forest cover is predominantly mature hemlock, trees whose size and stature defy the logging that once stripped the slopes. Commission Point, at 2.4 miles, is the first narrow finger south of Red Rock Bay. Its boat launching sites and day use areas make it a good alternate for the beginning of a walk along the shore.

Below the point, numerous little islands that choke the Narrows fill the water between the shore and the tip of the Tongue Mountain Range on the opposite shore. The steepest ledges of Erebus's shoulder crown almost to shoreline here. For 0.7 mile the shoreline swings to an almost east-west direction in the handsomest area of all, the approaches to Shelving Rock.

At 3.1 miles, the red trail to Shelving Rock forks left. South of that intersection the shore trail is marked with red and yellow, and there is a nice cool spring just south of the intersection. Look for a small spring house on the right, next to the shore.

The last 0.5 mile of the shore trail to a point above Pearl Point where the yellow trail takes off up the slopes of Shelving Rock is described in section 13.

19 Black Mountain Point to the Ponds and Lapland Intersection

Hiking, camping
3.1 miles, 2 hours, 1450-foot elevation change

The trail from Black Mountain Point to that mountain's tiny ponds follows a logging road whose base is at least 130 years old. There are places where the grade, even with the leveling effect of many switchbacks, seems too steep for horse and wagon.

The trail begins with red markers just to the north of Black Mountain Point, a destination accessible by water. It passes beside a field, the remnants of the front lawns of Horicon House, and heads in a northeasterly direction on a long traverse. At 0.45 mile you walk beneath ledges on stretches of washed-out roadway, here eroded to bedrock. At 0.9 mile you approach the edge of a deep ravine, a sheer face on the northern side. The 0.95 mile climb to the first switchback, 600 feet above the lake, takes at least half an hour.

The grade becomes much steeper as the trail turns away from the ravine. Steep traverses continue for 0.45 mile, climbing 400 feet, but the trail returns at the end of each traverse close enough to the stream to allow views of water cascading through the deep gorge. In many places the trail is worn to bedrock, and the rubble underfoot can be a hazard on the descent. In the next 0.4 mile, the trail curves away from the stream, swinging back to cross it at 1.85 miles. This last 0.9 mile segment, climbing 700 feet, could also take over half an hour.

The trail curves toward the north and, in less than 0.2 mile and a 200-foot climb, reaches an intersection 2 miles from Black Mountain Point. This intersection is often missed so watch for it carefully starting about 250 yards after crossing the stream. The way left, unmarked is the route to Black Mountain summit, section 22.

You want to continue right, east, on a yellow marked and less obvious trail. Less than ten minutes walking will cover the 0.3 mile to a rock shelf on the north side of the western pond. Here, at 2.3 miles, a lean-to is set back from the water, high on the shelf. The pond's shores are edged with marsh plants and woody shrubs, but the view from the raised ledge is quite pleasant.

The trail continuing east shows little sign of its origins as a logging road. The way is narrow and gently rolling as the trail swings north to avoid the marshes along the stream connecting the ponds. The traverse of hemlock covered knolls is most delightful, and the 0.45 mile to the second pond is less than a fifteen minute trek.

The eastern point, designated Round Pond on the DEC guideboards, is much smaller, with swampy shores around most of its circumference, but it is a gem. A huge beaver house is near the southern shore, and the stump of a tremendous pine stands on the northern shore, right beside the trail. As you walk farther east, beyond the pond, through the lovely flow at its inlet end, turn back for a view of the lower edge of the sharp face of Black Mountain.

The next 0.35 mile, to a point designated as the Lapland Pond Intersection, offers a very pretty walk, up and over one hemlock covered ridge, down into a ferny glen, and up a second ridge. It seems it takes but five minutes to cover the distance between your last glimpse of Round Pond and the intersection. From here you can either walk north, section 24, or south, section 26. If you choose to return to Black Mountain Point, the 3.1 mile walk, mostly downhill, will take an hour and twenty minutes. Before you head back, you could certainly enjoy a 0.2 mile walk north from the intersection, then 0.2 mile south on the eastern shore to Lapland Pond Lean-to.

20 East Shore Loop on Erebus

Hiking
5 miles, 3 hours, 1200-foot elevation change

Two surprisingly good views of Lake George are the highlights of this loop from Red Rock Bay. If you have a canoe, you can easily paddle to the shore of the bay and begin the walk on the east shore trail. Access by a larger boat requires starting from the day use dock at Commission Point, 0.4 mile south of the end of this loop, making the whole trip 5.8 miles long.

The loop is described in a clockwise direction, and no alternate starting is suggested because of one confusing intersection on the shoulder of Erebus. This loop shares 0.5 mile in common with the blue Vistas Trail, section 17. The southern end of the shared segment is well marked. The northern end is very difficult to spot the first time you try to find it.

At Red Rock Bay you can easily locate the yellow horse trail that heads southeast up the slopes of Erebus. This will be your return route. Walk north from this point on the shore trail, section 18, past Paradise Bay, to a second intersection at 0.9 mile where a horse trail, designated yellow but now only temporarily flagged, heads east-southeast up Erebus' slopes. Even this intersection is difficult to spot. The trail angles sharply back making an acute angle to the south with the shore trail. Look for a bunch of rocks near a curve in the shore trail. The intersection is here, in a thicket of small saplings.

The trail follows the route of an old logging road, climbing steeply beside a small stream. At 0.3 mile it crosses to the south side of the stream, then back again to the north at 0.5 mile. Now the trail becomes very steep, arcing north, and recrossing the stream. By the time the arc is complete, at 0.8 mile, the trail is heading south and you have already climbed 1100 feet from the lakeshore, 550 feet in the last 0.3 mile.

The end of the arc marks the end of the old road, which the trail has been following, and the newly cut yellow trail swings to the west of south. It descends a 3 foot ledge, then begins a long gentle climb.

Start looking for an obvious opening toward the lake. It is the signal to walk west 150 yards from the trail for the first view, one of the best from Erebus. It offers an expanse that covers more than three-fourths of the length of Lake George. The Tongue Mountain Range fills the opposite shore.

Beyond the overlook, you continue on the gentle uphill, reaching, at 1.3 miles, a sharp pitch up a 30-foot ledge. Above it you enter a hemlock grove and angle east, uphill, through open hardwoods to a height-of-land. A sharp right turn takes you into a draw, and a short and steep descent through the developing valley ends at a trail intersection at 1.8 miles.

This intersection with the blue Vistas Trail is all but impossible to find when you are walking the Vistas loop. A left turn here, away from the sharp ledges on the right, leads to the red Shelving Rock Brook Trail. You go straight ahead, below the ledges, on the blue trail for the 0.5 mile segment this loop shares with the blue Vistas Trail, section 17. You wind southwest over a nose, then down through a stand of hemlock, making a sharp hairpin turn before reaching a marked intersection.

A sign points along the yellow trail you will follow for the 0.8 mile descent to lakeshore. The intersection is about 800 feet above water level. You traverse a level course east of north for a short distance on the yellow trail before it begins to descend through a series of switchbacks, gradually turning to the west-northwest. There are outcrops and ledges on the uphill side of the switchbacks. You continue the switchback descent for 0.4 mile to an overlook 500 feet above the lake. Your perch gives you a great vantage directly over the water, with Arrow Island appearing as if it were right below you. The rest of the Narrows' islands are framed by the Point of Tongue and Shelving Rock Mountain. A few feet farther along the yellow trail you reach a second overlook, not quite as good as the first, with the views here to the south.

Fortunately this trail was carefully built for hikers, or perhaps horsemen. Its construction surely dates to the time Knapp owned the land. You do appreciate the careful construction of switchbacks as you descend the next 500 feet in 0.4 mile, heading north of west through a small ravine.

You emerge on the shoreline of Red Rock Bay and your starting point, completing the 5 mile circuit.

21 Black Mountain Point to Bumps and Fishbrook Ponds

A long walk on Erebus
8.6 mile circuit, 5 hours, 1900-foot elevation change

Of all the trails on the slopes of Erebus, this one best exemplifies the mountain's character. This long walk makes an arduous 8.6 mile trip, refreshingly broken by visits to Bumps and Fishbrook ponds. For the entire distance traversed on Erebus' western slopes, the trail is buried without vista in the deep forests that shroud the mountain. The hiker should not expect otherwise, for Erebus' name means that infernal region of the center of the earth not penetrated by the sun's rays. The mythical Erebus was a place of shadows and mystery where few things grew, where no living thing could survive. The mountain's slopes are far from barren, but hikers will be overwhelmed by the dark cover, the lack of undergrowth, and by the paucity of variety of growing things on the forest floor. Even an admirer of magnificent trees might become satiated by the walk in unrelieved forest cover.

The trailhead, accessible by water, will serve both ends of the loop of Erebus. Begin at Black Mountain Point and walk south on the shore trail for 0.4 mile to an intersection. The trail up the slopes is marked with both red foot trail disks and yellow horse trail disks, but there is no guideboard to indicate the trail's destination. The trail obviously follows an old tote road, built up with boulders but now rocky underfoot, its eroded surface washed and exposed in the century since the road was used.

The trail immediately swings north to follow the valley of a small stream. After climbing 400 feet in 0.4 mile, you reach, at 0.8 mile, the first of several switchbacks that pulls away from the ravine into a deep grove of hemlock. Even the return switchback toward the ravine continues the steady climb. A second switchback leads into a mixed hardwood area, and the end of it signals a relatively level stretch. At about the 1100-foot level, openings through the trees reveal sharp cliffs on the opposite, northern, side of the ravine you are following. At the 1300-foot level, after 0.9 mile of climbing, you are aware that the valley you have been following is suddenly much broader. You are looking across a deep cleft on the side of Erebus, either side of which is drained by a stream. Your views are enhanced by the general lack of undergrowth. The total 1.3 miles to this point probably requires nearly an hour.

You reach a brook, which may be quite insignificant in summer, at 1.45 miles, and shortly thereafter you cross it. The trek continues less steeply for 0.45 mile to an intersection at 2 miles at 1900 feet in elevation. You will probably need an hour and twenty minutes to reach the intersection.

The return is via the trail you just climbed, but the rest of the walk is a loop, which is described in counterclockwise direction. The way straight ahead by which you will return leads in 0.5 mile to Fishbrook Pond. You should turn right, southwest, on a red-marked trail cut within the last decade. It is seldom used, and hardly seems appropriate for horses or snowmobiles for which it is designated.

The red trail continues to climb, but at a more moderate rate, rising 300 feet in 0.6 mile. Occasionally the route has the look of an old tote road. It is interesting that almost none of this trail follows the route of older trails shown on the 1890 series USGS maps.

It takes about twenty minutes to walk to a small draw where high ground rises on your right. Here, at 2.6 miles, the trail swings to a nearly southerly direction. A swale beyond the draw hosts many ferns, and is open enough so that you can see the tops of cliffs near the summit of Erebus. You continue south below the cliffs, and the draw closes into a ravine with the trail plunging through it.

Throughout this section of the walk you are aware of the pine-topped ridge of the summit of Erebus, and during the walk through the ravine you are tempted to think you see the end of the summit ridge, the steepest face of Erebus's triangular summit. At about 2000 feet, you are close beneath those cliffs. This point, at 3.15 miles, is reached after a forty minute walk from the intersection.

The red trail forks right, section 17, at an intersection at 3.4 miles. For the loop, take the yellow fork, left, for the stated 0.6 mile trek to Bumps Pond. The yellow trail describes a tortuous course, first crossing a log bridge, definitely unsuitable for horses, then traversing a nice dry ledge. You make a hairpin turn at the head of the draw, then contour along its eastern side, traversing the steep slope and heading almost due east for a time. The general direction of the zigzag course is east, then finally southeast.

You cross a height-of-land that is but five minutes or 0.15 mile from Bumps Pond. The trail is now routed along an obvious woods road. You pass a cement-walled, covered spring where you are within sight of the pond. At the pond, at 4 miles, turn north on the trail to the intersection at the foot of Bumps Pond where you continue north toward Fishbrook Pond, section 10.

You reach Fishbrook Pond at 5 miles. See section 27 for the 1.1 mile route along the east side. Take the left fork at the north end of the lake, pass the lean-to and continue around the shore to the northern tip of the pond. Continue nearly 0.5 mile, heading north of west through a draw, down to the intersection with the yellow marked trail. Here at 6.6 miles you begin the walk down the deeply wooded slopes back to Black Mountain Point. For the 8.6 mile circuit, allow two hours and forty minutes for the climb to Bumps Pond, another hour to reach the northwest corner of Fishbrook Pond, and about two hours for the return from Fishbrook Pond to Black Mountain Point.

22 Black Mountain
Hiking, distant views
2.8 miles, 2½ hours, 2320-foot elevation change

Black Mountain, at 2646 feet elevation, is the tallest of the mountains rimming Lake George. It is a guidepost to orient the horizon when seen from many places throughout the Adirondacks, and the views from its summit are really wonderful. Two trails reach the summit, and the trek from Black Mountain Point, with 2320 feet of climbing, is the more arduous and the more spectacular.

It has been a favorite climb since steamers first brought vacationers to the point in the first half of the nineteenth century. The trip, beginning originally on the logging road of section 19, was followed by a scramble up the steep southern face. A century ago visitors could secure a horse at Black Mountain Point for the trip. By then Cyrus Butler, the builder of Horicon Pavilion, had built a good trail to the summit. The zigzags up the last third of the climb were constructed to be safe for equestrians as well as hikers. It is the trail in use today but in the hotel days a toll was charged for its use, probably to defray the cost of building and maintenance. Hikers paid $1, riders $3.

The trip today is free, and the fact that the trail is in such good condition is due more to its superior construction than to modern maintenance.

Walk the first 2 miles of the red trail, section 19, from Black Mountain Point to the first intersection, which is 0.2 mile beyond a stream crossing. Take the left fork, and within 0.15 mile and 160 feet of ascent you reach a charming lookout with a view directly into Black Mountain Pond. Now a marvelous series of switchbacks begins. The trail is built tight beneath rock ledges. It twists and turns, climbing steeply for 0.55 mile before attaining an overlook at 2.6 miles. You gain nearly 600 feet in that segment. The only disappointment in this section is the lack of views, but those that greet you as you emerge on open rock below the windswept summit are more than ample reward. You can walk off to the west of the trail for the best views, overlooking Erebus and the islands that fill the Narrows. The deep trench fault of the lake is clearly delineated below you. Wind-shaped and twisted cherries, maples, and elderberries cling tenaciously to the rocky summit.

Turn east and climb again to approach the tower from the southwest. You will find the ranger's cabin west of the tower and a picnic table near the foot of the tower.

The views south are best from the first opening, unless you choose to climb the tower for the full panorama. From the rocks below the tower you overlook the Tongue Mountain Range, a view that always impresses me with the tortuous course of its range trail. Five Mile Mountain, Fifth Peak, the two unnamed knobs, French Point Mountain, and First Peak are clearly identified as the range drops off to Montcalm Point.

North of Black, on the east shore of Lake George, lies Elephant, with the profile of Anthony's Nose unmistakable beyond. North of Anthony's Nose, on the west shore, the sharp slopes of Rogers Rock are visible. South of the Rock you can pick out Hague, Silver Bay, and Sabbath Day Point, which lies just north of the Tongue Mountain Range.

Lying beyond the Tongue Mountain Range, on the horizon defined by the narrow segment outlined by the valley between Five Mile Mountain and Fifth Peak and the summit of Five Mile Mountain itself, lies a wonder of mountains to identify. Blue Mountain is over the valley, with Vanderwhacker, Santanoni, and Hoffman north, to the right of it. Next lies Pharaoh, with Macomb and Dix on the horizon behind. Continuing now to the left, on a clear day you can distinguish Basin, Skylight, Marcy, and Redfield. To the right of the Tongue Mountain Range, Giant and Rocky Peak Ridge are visible on the horizon.

The tower permits good views of the Green Mountains east of Lake Champlain. The observer, whose days off are Thursday and Friday, should be able to help you identify other mountains in the skyline. The return is much more rapid, so that about four hours is required for the trip, but do allow time to enjoy the summit.

Rattlesnake dens are to be found in the cliffs below the summit; and peregrine falcons have nested there and may again if undisturbed.

Pike Brook Road

THE PIKE BROOK Trailhead is at the far northeastern corner of the state lands that border Lake George's eastern shore. From the north and Northway Exit 28, go east on NY 74 to Ticonderoga and south on NY 22 to Clemons, turning west there toward Huletts Landing. From the south and Northway Exit 20, go north briefly on NY 9 and turn east on NY 149 to Fort Ann. Here you turn north on US 4 to Comstock, where the road north is designated both as US 4 and NY 22. South of Whitehall, US 4 forks east. Continue north on NY 22 as it follows the Champlain Valley to Clemons, where you turn west toward Huletts Landing. Follow the road toward Huletts Landing for 2.6 miles and turn south on Pike Brook Road for 0.8 mile to the marked trailhead.

Fishermen use this trailhead because it offers the shortest and easiest treks to the interior ponds. Only Millman Pond so far is classified acid critical. Six interior ponds are regularly stocked with brook trout and fishing is especially good at Fishbrook Pond.

23 Black Mountain from the East

Hiking, snowshoeing
2.2 miles, 2 hours, 1100-foot elevation change

Both the walk to the summit of Black Mountain from Pike Brook Trailhead and the climb are shorter than the trek from the lakeshore, sections 19 and 22. The Pike Brook Trailhead is 800 feet higher than the lake.

The red-marked trail begins along a gravel road that leads in 0.7 mile to a private residence. The tower is visible across the fields beyond the farmhouse. The trail follows the right side of the fields leading up into the woods. A blue trail forks left at an intersection 0.3 mile farther. It should take no more than half an hour to reach the intersection at 1 mile.

You continue on the red trail following an old tote road now edged with deep woods flowers, arbutus, and foamflower. A second intersection is reached 0.2 mile farther. Here the snowmobile trail loops north to rejoin the red trail at 1.6 miles. The trails immediately split again with the snowmobile trail again looping north. Both trails join again just below the last pitch approaching the summit. The lower grade of the snowmobile trail is attractive for those who want to snowshoe the mountain in winter.

The red hiking trail turns sharply left up the hillside at the junction at 1.6 miles, near a small stream. The trail now follows the stream, climbing rather steeply to a rock ledge over which water trickles down to join the stream. Then the trail turns away from the stream and climbs the ledge, traversing bedrock along it.

Beyond it an area of severe blowdowns provides some openings through which you can see Knob Hill. The trail climbs toward the summit through a small draw until that draw becomes too steep. There, at nearly 2 miles, a little less than 0.2 mile from the summit, the trail swings southeast, traversing below the steepest ledges, then turns sharply to climb the summit from the east along a gentler ridge.

You will find picnic tables, two ranger cabins, and the fire tower. Note the continuing red trail south to Black Mountain Point. The description of that trail, section 22, also contains details of the panorama from the summit.

24 Lapland Pond

Hiking, camping
2.1 miles, 1 hour, minimal elevation change

Lapland Pond is one of the prettier ponds nestled high in the mountain range on Lake George's eastern shore. A small hill on the northwest drops cleanly to the water, making a high and dry shoreline. A lean-to sits atop a rock ledge about a third of the way south along the eastern shore.

From the Pike Brook Trailhead, walk west as to Black Mountain, section 23, continuing beyond the farmhouse to the first intersection at 1 mile. Here turn south on the blue marked trail. This, too, was an old tote road. You pass a bog meadow and walk along a hemlock knoll. Because of beaver activity, the trail here has been displaced to the east onto higher ground. There is a bridge over an intermittent stream and then the trail curves to the right entering a draw at 1.5 miles. The rest of the way, 0.6 mile, is through a broad level saddle between Black Mountain and a small hill. In this level section, water is held on the trail, making walking difficult. The second-growth forest of beech and maple does not always shade the trail.

The walking is so easy, you need less than an hour to reach the intersection north of the pond. The trail left leads 0.2 mile to the lean-to. The way right leads 0.2 mile to Lapland Pond Intersection, section 19.

25 Black Mountain Loop

Hiking, views
6.4 miles, 6 hours, 1100-foot elevation change

A superior one day loop can be walked by combining the 2.2 mile trek up Black Mountain, section 23, a descent via 0.8 mile of the western trail, section 22, the walk east past the ponds to Lapland Intersection, the last 1.1 miles of section 19, a 0.2 mile trek north to connect with the Lapland Pond Trail of section 24, and finally a 2.1 mile return walk on the Lapland Pond Trail. The entire loop, with detours for views and a stop at the lean-to, excursions that add at least a mile, can be walked comfortably in six hours.

If you are walking this loop in the counterclockwise direction, one intersection may not be obvious—the turn from the southern Black Mountain Trail to head toward the Lapland Intersection. That intersection is only 0.15 mile below the Black Mountain Pond overlook, and if you miss it and get as far as the brook crossing, turn around and go back 0.2 mile to search for it.

26 Millman Pond

Hiking, camping
3.3 miles from Pike Brook Road, 1 hour 40 minutes, 400-foot elevation change

This description of the yellow trail to Millman Pond picks up from the Lapland Pond Intersection, section 24. Adding 1 mile to that walk, not the 1.9 miles the sign says, you can reach the lean-to on Millman in a little over 2 hours with a pack.

South of the Lapland Intersection you pass a flow across which part of Lapland Pond is visible. The flow continues to the east of the trail. Enormous stumps from logging days remain. The marsh, along the outlet of Millman Pond, is a wild stump forest, trees killed by beaver flooding some time ago. After a fifteen minute walk south of the intersection, a 0.5 mile arc around the flow, a snowmobile trail angles back left. Its destination is a trailhead on private land to the southeast.

Continuing on the yellow trail (do not be surprised to see red markers as well), the trail begins a steady and moderate ascent. The route is across the outlet stream to the west side, then back within 100 yards to a hop-a-stone crossing. Now the trail follows the outlet closely, for the valley is very narrow. As you climb high to the hemlock covered bank above the outlet stream, watch for the stump of an unusually large pine. The snowmobile trail, which only made one crossing, now rejoins the hiking trail, and within 200 yards both arrive at the outlet.

Millman Pond is a nice surprise. A very small beaver dam at its narrow outlet does a surprising job of raising the water level. There is a beautiful view across the pond from the outlet end. The trail follows a very narrow ridge, perhaps an esker, on the east side of the pond. The ridge separates the pond from a beaver meadow to the east that lies at a slightly higher elevation. A lean-to with a fireplace crowns the ridge; the view west from the lean-to is over the pond and the view east is across a stump forest that is home to many birds. Walk east along the shore to discover a large beaver house tucked almost below the shore, just a couple feet from it. The whole pond is only 0.3 mile long and very narrow, but a handsome place to camp.

27 Fishbrook and Greenland Ponds

Hiking, camping, fishing
4.3 miles from Pike Brook Road, 2½ hours, 200-foot elevation change

Fishbrook is certainly the best of the upland ponds, with a very handsome dry shoreline. Its two lean-tos and a camping spot on a peninsula that juts out from the southwestern corner are well used. To reach Fishbrook from Millman Pond, you climb 100 feet to a saddle and descend 200 feet in a 1-mile walk that should take about half an hour, following the yellow trail all the way.

Walk 0.1 mile south of the lean-to on Millman Pond, section 26, to the swampy southern shore. Here you start to climb to the southwest to a height-of-land, reached at 0.3 mile. You cross a small draw, then contour to the east around an unnamed hill. After you have nearly completed the descent to Fishbrook, you pass an intersection with the red trail that leads 1 mile east down the slopes to Greenland Pond. There is a second intersection 100 yards farther, almost at the lake shore. The way right, west, leads 0.2 mile to a lean-to, 0.5 mile to the northern corner of the pond, and 2.5 miles to Black Mountain Point, section 21.

The lean-to on the northern promontory sits above a long triangular rock ledge that slides gradually to the water. The view of the east face

Lake George from Erebus Mountain

of Erebus above the pond is quite handsome. Swimming from the long rock finger is good.

A red trail with both red and yellow markers continues south from the intersection, traversing the eastern shore of the pond. At the southeastern corner of the lake, 0.3 mile south, you pass an intersection with an abandoned snowmobile trail that leads across both state and private land to Fish Hill near Great South Bay on Lake Champlain.

Walking around the south shore of Fishbrook Pond you reach a second lean-to on a promontory, a spot as handsome as the first. To the west of this lean-to there is a good campsite jutting out into the water. At 4.9 miles from Pike Brook Road you intersect the yellow trail from Bumps Pond, section 10.

The 1 mile walk from the northeastern corner of Fishbrook Pond to Greenland Pond is marked as a snowmobile trail. Greenland's swamps are not conducive to camping; in spring and summer it is most often frequented by fishermen. The continuing route east to NY 22, which had been marked as a snowmobile trail is now closed as it leads to private lands.

28 The Long Walks

The honeycomb of trails on the east shore of Lake George offers an endless number of permutations and combinations. For those who want to backpack on longer trips, here is a sample of the best routes.

From Pike Brook Road, you can walk to the summit of Black Mountain, down to lake shore, and up via the Erebus Trail, section 21, to Fishbrook Pond, with the return via Millman and Lapland Ponds.

The longest hike from Pike Brook Trailhead would take you up and over Black Mountain, down to lake shore, along to Shelving Rock and up to its summit. From the intersection below Shelving Rock's summit, there are four ways to get to Bumps Pond, two involving treks through Dacy Clearing, from which you can reach Bumps Pond by detouring to the summit of Sleeping Beauty. These circuits can be made either by starting on the shore of Lake George or from the Shelving Rock Trailhead.

From the main DEC trailhead you can walk north to Dacy Clearing, directly up to Bumps Pond, or via Sleeping Beauty, and head northwest to the intersection with the red Shelving Rock Brook Trail. A long trek along the shoulder of Erebus toward Shelving Rock is a great extension of this walk. You finish the trek by either of the two routes toward Dacy Clearing.

A tremendous walk from Dacy Clearing heads west along Dacy Clearing Road, climbs Shelving Rock, descends via the yellow trail to Lake George, and then treks north to the yellow trail, section 20. From there climb the slopes of Erebus again and head southwest on the blue trail past the overlook to descend on the yellow trail to the Shelving Rock Brook Trail, part of which you would use for your return to Dacy Clearing.

Another great trek starting from the main DEC parking area is the circuit of Sleeping Beauty, Bumps Pond, and its overlook north to Fishbrook to camp, then back south on the shoulder of Erebus to follow its ridge line all the way to Shelving Rock where, again, a number of alternates can be used to return to the parking area.

A shorter circuit involves exploring all of Shelving Rock from the falls northeast to Bumps Pond, returning via Sleeping Beauty and one of the trails from Dacy Clearing.

Most of the section references are omitted from the above trips. The best way to plan a long backpacking trip in the area would be first to become acquainted with the trailheads and a few of the interior destinations and then to chart your own course. The eighty miles of trails described are more than enough for a week-long backpacking trek, and the vistas and ponds are ample reward. For the best overnight camping, your circuits should involve one of the fine lean-tos on Fishbrook, Millman, Lapland, and Black Mountain ponds.

Tongue Mountain Range

THE TONGUE MOUNTAIN Range is a geologically interesting 10 mile long chain of mountains thrusting south into Lake George and almost parallel to the major axis of the lake. The great triangular block fault is upraised between diverging fault fractures. The western fault line borders Northwest Bay; the eastern fault faces the lake spanning the middle of the lake's thirty-two-mile length; and the intersection of the fault lines is the Point of Tongue, or Montcalm Point. This apex touches the lake at the southern end of the island-filled Narrows. At one time Tongue Mountain probably separated the lake into its two ancient predecessors.

The Range is composed of syenite, mostly quartz bearing, exposed in many places in sheer cliffs along the eastern scarp. The lake shores touched by the range are so precipitous that only a few cottages were ever built there. With the exception of a small segment of private property on the bay side and a cluster of cottages on Turtle Bay and another opposite the southern end of Turtle Island, the entire range is state land. Its slopes and lack of water prohibited other settlements, but not the logger's ax. As on the shores farther north toward Hague, the logging days were early in the nineteenth century. Softwood was floated to the sawmills at Ticonderoga, as many as 10,000 logs a year as late as 1860. Hardwoods, too, were harvested, to be turned to charcoal for the ravenous iron forges on Lake Champlain. Oak was cut for barrel staves. Not all the logs made their way to Ticonderoga, for often a sunken oak log can be seen through the lake's clear water, a number of these in Northwest Bay.

The Tongue Mountain Range is a place of many natural wonders; its slopes are great vantages from which to watch migrating warblers in spring or soaring hawks in summer. Its reptile population is infamous, for many rattlesnakes nest in crevices along the cliffs. It is wise to wear heavy boots and to watch where you place your hands. The threat of rattlers should not deter you from hiking, but it should make you wary. The Range is well known for the variety of wildflowers on its slopes, fields of trailing arbutus near the summits, and such a plethora of spring blooming flowers that hikers in early May often see more than three dozen different species.

There are only two roadside trailheads for the hikes on Tongue Mountain. To find either, head east from Northway Exit 24, following the signs toward Bolton. As you approach the lake and NY 9N, the range is visible to the northeast. Turn north on NY 9N for 3.7 miles to an excellent canoe launching site and parking area on the east side of the highway. At 3.75 miles there is a bridge over Northwest Bay Brook, and 0.15 mile farther is the Clay Meadow Trailhead. The parking for that trailhead is at 4 miles in an abandoned quarry beside the road. At the end of the day you can soak tired feet in the quarry pond and study the columnar jointing in the dark red gabbro on the far side of the quarry.

If you continue north on NY 9N, you will pass a picnic area with a good spring. It is in a reforestation area on the west side of the highway. The highway climbs, now heading east, and crosses the base of the Tongue Mountain peninsula at 1091 feet elevation. It then descends, reaching the parking area for the Deer Leap-Five Mile Mountain Trailhead, which is on the north side of the road at 9 miles.

Two other trailheads are accessible by water, one at Montcalm Point, and one at Five Mile Mountain Point. There is no dock facility at the present near the latter, but there is a good, protected state dock just north of Montcalm Point in the Narrows.

29 Deer Leap

Hiking, snowshoeing, picnicking
1.6 miles, 1 hour, minimal elevation change

A hike to Deer Leap and return is the easiest of the walks that you can make on the Tongue Mountain Range. On the south side of the highway, opposite the northern parking area, a dirt road heads west, paralleling the highway. In 0.1 mile the blue marked trail turns south. The trail follows an old horse trail, well built up with sizeable stones by the Civilian Conservation Corps. After a gentle rise, at 0.5 mile you will find an outhouse on the right hand side of the trail.

You reach the height-of-land for this trek at 0.55 mile, after climbing 300 feet, a walk of less than fifteen minutes. A trail intersection marks

From Deer Leap

the height-of-land: the way right, south, leads to Five Mile Mountain and the Tip of the Tongue, Montcalm Point, which the DEC guideboard calls Point of Tongue, at 9.85 miles. A yellow branch trail leads straight ahead, east, 1.05 miles to Deer Leap.

The height-of-land defines the transition from the tall hardwood forests of the western slopes to the scrubbier oaks and pines of the eastern slopes. Beyond the intersection you cross the brow of a small ridge, quickly beginning to descend. You will see a path leading to an occluded overlook after only a short walk of 230 yards past the intersection. A second path, this one with a yellow marker, forks right at 0.83 mile. This leads to the best overlook in the entire walk. To enjoy it, walk southwest for about 100 yards, keeping a level contour across the open area. The view southwest is across the islands of the Narrows to Shelving Rock, and south to Black Mountain across the Mother Bunch Islands. The round top of Sugarloaf lies southeast. To your left, twisted pines outline the southern prong of the Deer Leap promontory. Do not forget to look about in the small patches of moss between the open rock slabs. They are home to lady's slippers in late spring and ladies' tresses orchids in late summer. Rusty woodsia is the tiny fern that likes the steepest places.

Returning to the trail, you continue the descent 0.16 mile into a valley and wind across it and up to a ridge at 1.1 miles. From the ridge you can look back along the range to Five Mile Mountain and this view clearly delineates the cirque below you that opens up into Davis Bay. Continue across the ridgeline for 0.2 mile, passing a faint path right to a small overlook. For 0.2 mile you descend again, with good views north to the east-west facing fault scarp of Bloomer's cliffs. You cross another nose in the ridgeline, still descending, and finally reach a partially wooded overlook at 1.6 miles. You will discover that trees are beginning to obstruct the view, which is across to Huletts Landing with Elephant and Black Mountain stretching south. From here Black Mountain presents its most imposing profile. Before you turn back, walk around the open patches south of the trail. You will not find a better view along the wooded cliff top of Deer Leap, but you may find ebony spleenwort, a dainty little fern, filling small crevices in the rock.

For all the winding up and down the ridgeline you have done, your destination is at the same elevation as the start; you pass a height-of-land at 1380 feet. Two hours will suffice for the round trip, and if you only have an hour or so to spare you can easily walk to the first overlook in that time.

30 Five Mile Mountain from the North
Hiking, snowshoeing, camping
3.6 miles, 2 hours, 1190-foot elevation change

Walk the first 0.55 mile as for the trail to Deer Leap, section 29. At the intersection turn sharply right, heading south, and continue on the blue trail. You immediately begin to climb at a moderate rate, passing some open ledges, but staying mostly in fairly deep woods with a few significant pines. You are following a very narrow ridgeline that drops off sharply on both sides. The route becomes less steep, passing a stand of really big hemlock, at 1.1 miles, then begins the steep ascent again. You angle toward the lake at 1.2 miles, and again you are climbing fairly steeply. You reach a small overlook summit of Brown Mountain at 1.45 mile, a climb of 900 feet from the road and a fifty-minute walk.

After a short descent from Brown's summit, you continue walking along the ridge. The section at 1.7 miles is mostly level, pleasant and open, with blueberries, some big red pine, trailing arbutus, and twisted stalk for company. At 1.75 miles you cross a three-log bridge to a ledge with a lookout through the trees toward Northwest Bay. Lady's slippers dot the moss between open rock ledges. Blue arrows on the rocks or cairns lead the way. Notice the three-leaf cinquefoil, more commonly seen in the High Peaks.

You climb again at 2.05 miles, this time with birch and red, scotch, and white pine. This stretch always seems to be the nicest part of the trip, and if you pause you usually find many birds darting among the evergreens. One more steep pitch awaits, then an open patch that leads at 2.45 miles to the lean-to. From the lean-to you can see the range of hills across Northwest Bay.

The trail is a narrow footpath carved to bedrock in the thin soil where it winds below the lean-to and passes to the south of it. The trail arcs south as it enters the woods again. You wind across a small knob that is only 24 feet lower than the summit of Five Mile Mountain, and at 2.7 miles descend from the knob, making a hairpin turn around the end of a small draw. You continue contouring along the ridge, then at 2.9 miles you climb again. At 3.1 miles you reach a sign in the woods, not at an intersection. The distance to the lean-to you just passed is given erroneously. Also the stated 0.45 mile distance to the summit is correct for a lovely overlook to the east that is 0.25 mile beyond the summit.

The trail makes a sharp zigzag, then enters a very small draw in 0.2 mile. This draw is directly east of the summit and a good place to leave the trail to climb the last 20 feet to the long exposed rock that is Five Mile Mountain's true summit at 2256 feet. From the southwestern corner of the summit ridge, about 100 yards off the trail and 200 feet from the bench mark, there is a fine view across Northwest Bay Brook and south toward Prospect Mountain.

If you continue on the trail for 0.25 mile, a six-minute walk takes you on a hairpin loop south and around the head of a second draw, then across a ridge to the eastern overlook on top of a steep ledge. The views both up and down the lake are lovely, but from here intervening hills in the range make it impossible to see the Point of Tongue.

You can return to your car in an easy two hours. But if you have arranged a second car at Clay Meadow, sections 32 and 33 (many groups of hikers do this in order to enjoy a loop walk), the return via the southern approach is 3.5 miles long with a descent of 1829 feet and takes about the same time as the descent to the north.

31 Falls on Northwest Bay Brook
Picnicking

Northwest Bay Brook makes a sharp hook north in a narrow gorge just north of the NY 9N bridge over the brook. In that short space the brook is funneled through a deep, hemlock covered ravine. Either walk southwest opposite the parking area for Clay Meadow or walk south to the bridge and follow the brook upstream to the falls. You will find a delightful ten minute trek to a picnic spot or a place to muse where the roar of water drowns out all civilized sounds.

Falls on Northwest Bay Brook

32 Clay Meadow to the Ridgeline of the Tongue Mountain Range

Hiking, camping
1.9 miles, 1 to 1¼ hours, 1080-foot elevation change

This hour long climb on a red trail takes you to a trail intersection from which you can make the steep descent east to Lake George, section 34, or turn north to Five Mile Mountain, section 33, or south to French Point Mountain and Montcalm Point, section 35.

The trail begins south of the old quarry parking area and leads directly through tall red pines of the reforestation area. You cross a finger of Northwest Bay and reach an intersection at 0.4 mile. The way right leads to Point of Tongue. You head straight ahead, uphill, on a well-worn trail, with few red trail markers to guide you. The trail follows the valley of a small stream with a lovely waterfall. Leave the trail five minutes beyond the intersection and walk right toward the stream to see it.

In the next 0.9 mile the climb grows increasingly steep, crossing three bridges, two over intermittent streams. Ledges on your left at 1.3 miles indicate a sharp left turn to a switchback leading to the last steep pitch below a plateau.

The trail arcs south around the hemlock marsh that fills the plateau, then crosses the stream, without benefit of a bridge, and momentarily begins to climb again on a very sharp switchback. This last pitch at 1.5 miles takes you up 160 feet to the saddle between Five Mile Mountain and Fifth Peak. The trail intersection at 1.9 miles is just west of the high point of the saddle.

33 Five Mile Mountain from the South

Hiking, camping
3.25 miles, 2 hours, 1856-foot elevation change

Most hikers approach Five Mile Mountain from the north, making a return on the same trail or descending via the southern trail on a loop that requires two cars, section 30. This section describes the 1.35-mile, 776-foot climb from the intersection on the ridgeline, section 32, to the summit of Five Mile Mountain.

Turn left, north, at the intersection, on the blue trail, and shortly begin to climb. The way is steep, and you cover 400 feet in 0.4 mile, with several switchbacks to ease the grade. You are east across a long level nose, then at 0.9 mile you begin to climb again. You reach a small ridge at 1.15 miles, cross a small draw, then find the last 0.2 mile is a steep pitch to the ridgeline facing east. Here, there are views both north and south over the lake.

34 Five Mile Mountain Point

Hiking
1.35 miles from the ridgeline, 1 hour, 1140-foot elevation change

A red trail descends 1140 feet from the ridgeline intersection to water level at Five Mile Mountain Point, just north of Cathedral Bay. At present there is no dock at water level, but the round-trip, a two-hour walk, after a climb from Clay Meadow, makes quite an exciting hike. In places the grade is quite precipitous. Do remember that this trail crosses ledges where you must watch out for rattlesnakes.

You head east from the intersection, making at first a very gradual descent. You can see Black Mountain through the trees as the descent quickens. At 0.2 mile, you begin a very sharp descent followed by a more gradual section that ends at 0.5 mile.

As you begin the next steep descent at 0.6 mile, there are views of the lake and Black, Erebus, Sleeping Beauty, and Buck mountains. The trail again becomes more gradual, but that is only a relative description, for the entire way is quite steep.

After an half hour descent, at 0.9 mile, you are only 0.45 mile from lakeshore, but still 600 feet above it. The trail now begins a series of switchbacks with rock shoring on the outside of the trail. Stop for a breather three minutes along the switchbacks, for there is a superb picture spot from which you can see Huletts Landing. There is no view of the landing from the lakeshore. Here, you also have the best overlook of the Mother Bunch Islands, clearly separated as islands and not just bits of land jutting out from the opposite shore. The cliffs that fall to waterline are here seen to loom above and to your left.

At the end of forty minutes you reach a rocky point looking directly across the lake at Black Mountain, which seems to thrust straight out of the lake. To the north, you see Deer Leap, Sabbath Day Point, Harbor Island, and Spruce Mountain.

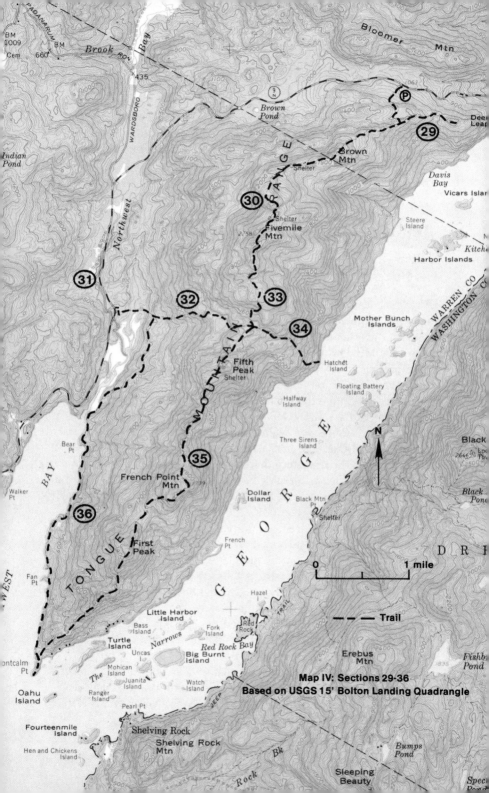

Map IV: Sections 29-36
Based on USGS 15' Bolton Landing Quadrangle

--- Trail

N

0   1 mile

35 Tongue Mountain Range to Montcalm Point or the Point of Tongue

Hiking, camping
5.8 miles from the ridgeline, 4 hours, 3000-foot elevation change

The Range Trail south from the ridgeline intersection to Montcalm Point is the most delightful 5.8 miles of hiking imaginable. The best way to walk this section is as part of a 13.1-mile loop using the Clay Meadow Ridgeline Trail, section 32, and a walk along Northwest Bay, section 36, to complete the circuit. This is a strenuous hike, requiring 9 hours, but one of the best anywhere in the Adirondacks.

From the intersection on the ridgeline, turn right, south, on the blue trail, which climbs 300 feet in 0.55 mile to a trail intersection where a yellow spur leads left, 0.25 mile to the summit of Fifth Peak. There is a lean-to on the summit, but no water. This is one of the most popular destinations on the Tongue Mountain Range, partly because of a promontory beyond the lean-to from which you can see the High Peaks.

Either return to the blue trail via the yellow trail, or bushwhack west down the ledges below the lean-to to intersect the blue trail, which is easy to find as it winds between the high points on the ridge.

Beyond the intersection the blue trail circles west of Fifth Peak across a level to a jagged promontory. This section and all that follow show little sign of use, and occasionally your walk may be dependent on the trail markers for sometimes the foot tread is concealed. This is especially true in early spring or in late fall, times when the walk is most pleasant.

In 1985 a fire started by careless campers burned the east flanks of Fifth Peak, but only a small area of trail. That has now been carefully marked. These steep slopes have burned before, and there is very little topsoil. Oak leaves, which are slow to decompose, burn readily. The ridgeline is no place for open fires.

At the end of the level, you cross west on the ridge where there are excellent views of Northwest Bay and marshes at its northern end. At 1.5 miles, the roller-coaster range trail begins to live up to its reputation. The chute is a drop down a precipitous trail, loosing 350 feet in less than 0.25 mile. And the minute you hit bottom, the trail starts up again, this time to climb the first of the two unnamed knobs that separate Fifth Peak and French Point Mountain. That knob, at 1.9 miles, is 200 feet above the intervening valley. The ridge of the knob is partially open, offering some views.

Lake George Narrows from First Peak

Watch carefully for the turn below the first knob. You turn left, toward the lake, before beginning to climb the second. At 2.15 miles, you begin the sharp descent from the second knob, following the ridge line south for 0.4 mile, making a sharp turn toward the lake at 2.55 miles. In 0.2 mile you reach the summit of French Point Mountain, an area thrust toward the lake. This wonderful position, 1400 feet above the lake but only 0.5 mile from the shore, provides the best views in the entire chain of open summits. The view of Paradise Bay and the Narrows is superb. The hike, 2.75 miles past the ridgeline intersection takes about an hour and a half. The total from Clay Meadow, 4.65 miles, usually means it is lunch time, and no better spot can be found to view the lake's islands and surrounding mountains.

The blue trail continues south along the ridge line marked with paint daubs on bare rock, then crosses the western side in 0.2 mile for a view of Northwest Bay. You now have your first glimpse of the Point of Tongue, that point Montcalm had to round to attack Fort William Henry in his decisive victory in the summer of 1757 during the French and Indian War.

The trail descends toward the bay in as steep a section as is found along the range trail, then at 3.05 miles angles back toward the lake. A hairpin turn takes you southwest again, along the top of the ridge, with views almost continuous. This course continues around the head of a valley that drops to the lake, curving in 0.4 mile to begin the climb to First Peak. You reach First Peak at 3.75 miles; the 1 mile walk from French Point Mountain takes about forty minutes.

From First Peak the sweep of cliff line from French Point Mountain to the water is most dramatic, and there is a wonderful view of the islands in the Narrows.

Another wild descent follows, this one dropping 400 feet on the ridge line with views along most of the route. The rest of the 0.7 mile trek from First Peak's northern summit to the next peak in the chain is relatively level, but the course is along the top of the precipitous rock slide that drops toward Turtle Bay.

Beyond First Peak's southern summit, at 4.5 miles, the trail almost disappears in a chute that seems to overhang the water. The trail goes along the east side of the ridge to a small clearing, giving a last view of the lake. A climb over a low ridge follows; then a long descent southwest into a little valley precedes the last junction at 5.5 miles. The trail has dropped 750 feet in the mile preceding the intersection. Continue 0.3 mile past the trail intersection to Montcalm Point. The descent from French Point Mountain to the Point requires two hours.

36 Northwest Bay Trail

Hiking, camping, snowshoeing
5.4 miles, 2 hours, 200-foot elevation change

The Northwest Bay Trail links Clay Meadow with the Point of Tongue. This is a lovely, gentle trail in itself, and makes an excellent round-trip walk from Clay Meadow. Since it will most likely be walked as the last leg of the long trip over the range, it is here described from south to north.

Along the trail, you pass marshes of Northwest Bay, which are often filled with birds and ducks. The deeper, moister woods of the west slopes of Tongue Mountain host a different range of flowers and ferns than the dry, exposed ledges that the Range Trail follows. Most amazing is the size of the forest cover, in view of the fires that swept these western flanks in 1908, 1909, 1911, 1912, and 1914.

From the intersection 0.3 mile north of Montcalm Point, walk due north at lake level for 0.25 mile, then follow the trail uphill, circling 0.3 mile in order to avoid a private inholding. At 0.85 mile, the steep flanks of Tongue Mountain force the trail close to shore where it remains for the next 0.5 mile. You cross a small creek at 1.35 miles, turn sharply left to round a bay at 2 miles. Beyond, the trail follows the shoreline closely again. At 2.3 miles you cross a bridge near which you should find a moss-covered boulder that is home to maidenhair spleenwort.

The trail improves as you head north, with rock work of the old CCC constructed horse trails making a firm foundation. Deep hemlock stands cover the hillside. At 2.8 miles you cross the first of a pair of bridges over the streams that flow into the bay south of Bear Point. Beyond Bear Point the bay narrows to a small channel, but most if the time the trail is out of sight of water. At 3.7 miles the trail heads sharply east, climbing away from the marshes and cliffs that drop right down to the water. The trip up the mountainside and back to water level is just over 1 mile and takes about half an hour. In less than 0.2 mile, just short of 5 miles, you cross the stream that the red trail follows toward the saddle, and that bridge is just 200 feet short of the intersection with the red trail. Take a left turn on the red trail for the 0.4 mile to the trailhead.

Although it is not hard to make the 5.4 mile walk to Montcalm Point from Clay Meadow in two hours, the return this way after a trek over the range always seems to take longer.

37 Ferns and Flowers on the Tongue Mountain Range

In one walk on the Tongue Mountain Range it is easy to spot at least twenty of the commonest eastern ferns. In fact, the range is an ideal place to become acquainted with the ferns you will meet throughout the Adirondacks:

Osmunda: Royal, Cinnamon, and Interrupted
Matteuccia: Ostrich fern
Adiantum: Maidenhair
Onoclea: Sensitive fern
Rusty *Woodsia*
Polypodium: the rock fern
Polystichum: Christmas fern
Dennstaedia: hayscented fern
Asplenium: both ebony and maidenhair spleenwort
Thelypteris: marsh, long beech, and New York fern
Dryopteris: Spinulose woodferns, evergreen woodferns, and the marginal shieldfern
Athyrium: lady fern and silvery spleenwort

Because of the varied habitat, the list of flowers is quite extensive. The diversity of the site from marsh to exposed ledges is home to a wonderful array of plants. The list below is not meant to be complete; it merely suggests what you can easily spot while hiking. Those with stars can usually be found flowering on Tongue Mountain the first weekend in May, the height of the spring bloom:

Beech-drops, *Epifagus Virginiana*
Indian Pipe, *Monotropa uniflora*
Pine-drops, *Pterospora andromedea*
Pearly everlasting, *Anaphalis margaritacea*
*Quaker Ladies, *Houstonia caerulea*
*Northern Coralroot, *Corallorhiza trifida*

Nodding Ladies'-tresses, *Spiranthes cernua*
*Pale Corydalis, *Corydalis sempervirens*
Bristly Sarsaparilla, *Aralia hispida*
*Wild Sarsaparilla, *Aralia nudicaulis*
*Dwarf Ginseng, *Panax trifolius*
Princess Pine or Pipsissewa, *Chimaphila umbellate*
*Bunchberry, *Cornus canadensis*
Shinleaf, *Pyrola elliptica*
*Canada Mayflower, *Maianthemum canadense*
*Goldthread, *Coptis groenlandica*
Harebell, *Campanula rotundifolia*
*Rock Saxifrage, *Saxifraga virginiensis*
*Pussytoes, *Antennaria neglecta*
*Pink Lady's-slippers, *Cypripedium acaule*
*Hooked Buttercup, *Ranunculus recurvatus*
*Trailing Arbutus, *Epigaea repens*
*Wintergreen, *Gaultheria procumbens*
*Dutchman's-breeches, *Dicentra cucullaria*
*Stink pots, *Trillium erectum*
*Painted Trillium, *Trillium undulatum*
*Gaywings, *Polygala paucifolia*
*Blue Cohosh, *Caulophyllum thalictroides*
*Many violets—Canada, Downy, White
*Starflower, *Trientalis borealis*
Twinflower, *Linnaea borealis*
*Dogtooth-Violet, *Erythronium americanum*
*Bellwort, *Uvularia grandiflora*
*Wild-oats, *Uvularia sessilifolia*
*Twisted Stalk, *Streptopus roseus*
*Solomon's-Seal, *Polygonatum biflorum*
*Bead Lily, *Clintonia borealis*
*Three-toothed Cinquefoil, *Potentilla tridentata*
*Spring Beauty, *Claytonia virginica*
*May flower, *Hepatica americana* and *acutiloba*
*Miterwort, *Mitella diphylla*
*Foamflower, *Tiarella cordifolia*
*Marsh-marigold or cowslip, *Caltha palustris*
Baneberries, red and doll's-eyes, *Actaea*
*Wild Columbine, *Aquilegia canadensis*

  Shrubs and trees in bloom in May:

Blueberries	Shad-bush
Cherry	Early Honeysuckle

Bolton-Hague Tract

HAGUE IS SO isolated by the steep hills that surround it that for many years the community's traffic and trade were carried out principally over Lake George and along its outlet to Ticonderoga. The section of road north from Bolton over the Tongue Mountain Range to Hague was used only for lumbering in the late 1880s and was not considered a passable highway until this century. For years, the road from Bolton north to Hague followed Northwest Bay Brook, winding northeast through a series of high valleys to a height of 1400 feet above Lake George, and finally dropping east along Battle Hill Road toward Hague. That old thoroughfare is called Wardsboro Road after the tiny settlement near its southern end.

Most of Wardsboro Road and its northern connectors are now abandoned and labeled as snowmobile trails. A walk along the abandoned roadway offers hikers a delightful way to explore the deep interior and a great opportunity to discover a multitude of wild flowers.

At the southern end, Wardsboro Road traverses a broad, fertile valley, first settled in the 1820s by William Ward. His son, born in 1826, was the first white child born in the valley. By 1858, twenty-three farms, two saw mills, and two schoolhouses were strung out along the road. In winter, logs were hauled south to Lake George. A stage made a weekly round trip along the road from Bolton, through the valley to Graphite, and down to Hague.

But this fertile valley could not compete with the western plains, and the population of the valley dwindled. A notable exception was E. H. Meyer's Alma Farm where Jersey cows were raised from 1870 to 1920. The farm became a CCC Camp, and reforestation plantations of pine now fill the abandoned fields.

38 Catamount Cliffs
Snowshoe bushwhack

The first adventure north of the Tongue is on a mountain that very much resembles the peaks of that range. Catamount has steep cliffs and cliff top views, though its summit is wooded. From the lean-to on Five Mile Mountain, Catamount appears as a long ridge with a cliffy outcrop on the west

(39)

H A G U E

Indian Mtn

Little Jabe Pond

(50)

Jabe Pond

Middle Mtn

Brook

No 108 Mtn

JEEP

0   1 mile

——— Trail
•••••••• Bushwhack
——— Road

N

Catamount Mtn

RONDACK   S T A T E   P A R K

Map V: Sections 29, 38-39, 50

Based on USGS 7½′ Silver Bay Quadrangle

(38)

B l o o m e r   M o u n t a i n

Sabbath

BM 1091

9N

P BM 1065

BM 461

Brown Pond

(29)

Deer Leap

ANGE

Brown Mtn

end. You can see little of this from NY 9N because the long ridge of Bloomer Mountain lies between Catamount and the road. But for a preview of what you are to climb, watch carefully as you head north on 9N from Bolton. After the road crosses Northwest Bay Brook, it makes a sweeping curve to the right through an alder swamp, just before it begins to climb Tongue Mountain. As you start to cross the alder swamp, you get a brief glimpse at the mountain that is right ahead of you with the cliffs on the left end of the ridge.

Catamount has many cliffy places and the circuitous route described is designed to avoid them as well as offer varied scenery and terrain. It goes over a knob at the end of Bloomer, then down across a swampy valley and finally up and onto Catamount. More direct routes may exist, but they might be difficult on snowshoes. If you tried this route in summer, you would have trouble with the swamp and especially with the knob on Bloomer with its broken rock that is such a great habitat for rattlesnakes.

Start on the top of the rise after the first dip in the road west of the Deer Leap Trail, section 29. Since there is no parking here, unless the road is widely plowed, you may have to continue east to the turnout for Deer Leap to park. From the start, head north for the end of Bloomer Mountain passing a beaver pond a short distance from the road. In case you might be tempted to try the cliffs on Bloomer that rise above you here, think twice. Local folklore tells of a number of deaths on these cliffs; there is no ledge on the way to the top, and they are not very high so any view is blocked by Brown Mountain and the Tongue Mountain Range. However, the end of Bloomer is spectacular with bare rock coming steeply down into the valley.

Round the cliffs, winding just east of north to a saddle on the knob. There is a lower saddle to the east, but the approach is much steeper. As it is, this is the toughest part of the climb. When you round the cliffs on Bloomer, you can see the left peak of the knob ahead of you; traverse toward it but east of it, through the saddle.

From the saddle head about 50° magnetic; this will take you along a tiny stream, which will be invisible in deep snow. Cross the swampy area at the base of the knob and head more easterly, looking for a little ravine between the steep end of the mountain and a small knob on its southeast flank. This is a distinctive landmark, and you have to find it to make sure you are on the right route.

Go through the ravine, then turn north again, then west, into a small valley that does not show on the topo map. This is the easiest route to the ridge and you will turn northwest when you reach it so you can follow it to a high point. From this high point, descend no more than ten feet, and bear slightly left, along a level, heading just north of west. If you begin to climb, you are probably headed in the wrong direction toward Catamount's summit.

The way west opens up into a broad plateau with a steep rise on the right and a drop on the left. Continue in the same direction, and gradually you will start to climb again. After a moderate climb there is a ridge ahead of you; the view, at the top of the cliff, is on the left end of the ridge. The view from the cliff is spectacular. Directly ahead, and a couple hundred feet below you is another knob of the mountain with a 500-foot cliff going at right angles to the one you are on. Looking off in the distance you look down Northwest Bay. To the left of the bay are Brown and Five Mile mountains and farther left is Bloomer. If it is really clear, you can see the High Peaks from a point way around to the right end of the cliff-top.

39 Wardsboro Road

Hiking, cross-country skiing, snowshoeing
3.7 miles, 2 hours, 890-foot elevation change

To find Wardsboro Road, turn left, west, from NY 9N, 5.8 miles north of the intersection of NY 9N and County Route 11 at North Bolton. Padanarum Road forks left, west, 1.4 miles north of NY 9N. Wardsboro Road heads almost due north through abandoned fields and reforestation areas. Across the field you can glimpse the cliffs on Bloomer Mountain followed by a good view of the steep back of Catamount. The road becomes impassable to vehicles long before the end of the second section of private land that borders the road. Be careful to park on state land so as not to obstruct access to private lands.

State land touches the road near the Wardsboro Cemetery, 1.5 miles north of the intersection with Padanarum Road. There is a salmon nursery with special minimum limits on Northwest Bay Brook along the bank east of the cemetery. Park near here and walk north along the roadway between stone walls left by settlers from the middle of the 1800s. In 0.5 mile you reach a washed out bridge, and immediately beyond it there is a waterfall on Northwest Bay Brook with ledges and holes in a strange crumbly rock. Hemlock trees shelter the waterfall. Between the waterfall and the road you might spot the fallen trunk of a chestnut, felled in the 1910 blight. The long, thin grain of chestnut is distinctive.

The old road, improved to the standards of the 1800s, is still well built with a rock base. A really good bank of wildflowers edges the road as it

Bloomer Cliffs from Catamount Mountain

begins to climb. In spring you should spot bellwort, Dutchman's-breeches, tall Canada violets, blue cohosh, hepatica, dwarf ginseng, and many ferns. A house marks the last parcel of private land, 1.4 miles from the cemetery.

From this point north, snowmobile markers designate the road. Shortly you will hear a second stream, down on your right, and will cross it ten minutes later on a snowmobile bridge. The walk from the cemetery to the snowmobile bridge is 1.9 miles and should take about an hour. The road becomes wetter as it passes through a swampy area that is open enough to permit views, even in summer, both east and west, the former including Beech Mountain and its cliffs and Spruce Mountain. You climb again, reaching a second snowmobile bridge at 3.1 miles. The 1.2-mile walk between the bridges takes just over half an hour.

Beyond the second bridge, in an old beaver meadow on the west, you will find the ruins of a huge beaver house. Fifteen minutes and 0.5 mile past the bridge you will meet a trail intersection. Here at 3.7 miles you can turn either way. The right fork curves northeast around Beech Mountain as the roadway heads toward Hague. Sharp ledges and small cliffs that edge the mountain rise to the right of the trail. After a mile, you climb a bit more and reach the boundary of private land. The snowmobile trail descends over 400 feet, reaching Split Rock Road at 6.2 miles. The northern trailhead at Split Rock Road is west of Jabe Pond Road, section 48.

If you choose the left fork at the intersection, you will start to climb gently around the shoulder of an unnamed hill, then more steeply as the trail passes through a small draw. Near the head of the draw the snowmobile trail reaches private land, but the marked trail continues north, then northeast, about 2 miles past the intersection, where at 5.7 miles it joins Fly Brook Road. This road leads directly northeast to NY 8. A left turn at Fly Brook Road takes you to Swede Pond. This old roadway circles south of Swede Mountain and was in the nineteenth century the route of the main road from Brant Lake to Hague. Beaver dams and lack of clearing make walking the road hard going. In fact, in the western section on state land southwest of Swede Mountain, the roadway is barely visible.

The best part of the walk along Wardsboro Road is accomplished before the main trail intersection, so you might wish simply to return south retracing your steps to your car, an easy walk that takes under an hour and a half. In winter this trail and parts of both branches north are good for cross-country skiing.

40 Padanarum Road
Old road, picnicking

It is best to start exploring the ponds and abandoned settlements in the Wild Forest area bounded by Brant Lake, Hague, and North Bolton with a drive through and a short walk to two of the interior ponds.

The drive through will take you from North Bolton to Brant Lake. From the south, take Exit 24 from the Northway and head east toward Bolton on County Route 11. As you approach the intersection with NY 9N, you will see Padanarum Road, a north turn 100 yards short of the intersection. It is puzzling how a biblical name meaning "situated in a region of rivers" was transported to this wild mountain road.

You can follow Padanarum Road toward Brant Lake, but before you embark on a forest trip, take a short detour left, west, at 2 miles, turning onto North Bolton Road, for just short of a mile, then north, right, on New Vermont Road. Within 0.4 mile the road curves west and a rather incongruous structure will appear on your left, south. The valley here contains the Union College radio telescope, protected and all but concealed by surrounding hills. It is a strange sight in the Adirondacks. It is not open to the public.

Returning to Padanarum Road and proceeding north, you pass Trout Falls Road at 1.9 miles. Beyond, you can enjoy close up views of High Nopit and its cliffs rising across a lovely marsh. The road passes through the valley between High Nopit and Pole Hill, the mountains that profile a camel's hump when viewed from the peaks along Lake George.

Just over 3 miles past Trout Falls Road (mileages here are important, for the road signs are often missing), you reach Padanarum Spur, a left, west, fork. The spur is a seasonal road, not maintained from September 1 through April 1. The spur, a lovely narrow dirt road, climbs 1.8 miles through deep woods to the unmarked trailhead for Long and Island ponds, section 41.

Continuing west, the spur gradually improves, intersecting Haysburg Road 1.8 miles past the Long and Island Pond Trailhead. Here a right, north, turn for 2.2 miles takes you to a second fork right into Duell Hill Road, which drops sharply in 1.2 miles to NY 8 at Brant Lake, 2.5 miles east of Northway Exit 25.

Besides enjoying the quiet and perhaps easy walk along Padanarum Spur, there are more beautiful spots to explore along the eastern end of Padanarum Road. Continuing north past the junction with Padanarum Spur, Padanarum Road makes a sharp turn to the east in just over 0.4 mile. From this point, Padanarum Road drops 400 feet in 1.6 miles before intersecting Wardsboro Road. It follows Round Pond Brook for the entire distance and is quite close to three lovely waterfalls along the way. The westernmost falls is near a sharp bend and is located on private land. The middle falls is in a deep gorge, 0.3 mile from the bend, and it has a lovely picnic area. The eastern falls also has a picnic area, and it is just 0.2 mile from the intersection with Wardsboro Road.

41 Long and Island Ponds

Hiking, camping, cross-country skiing, snowshoeing
1.3 miles, 1 hour, minimal elevation change

This short, round trip walk to Long and Island ponds from the unmarked trailhead on Padanarum Spur is along a designated snowmobile trail that follows an old tote road. Section 40 details the route to the trailhead.

The trail heads north, and after a brief uphill, the road levels off through alternate stands of hemlock, big birch, and apple trees that once lined old fields. Two swampy areas lush with ferns also line the first 0.8 mile before state land is reached. Long Pond is but 0.4 mile farther. Within sight of the marshy southern end of Long Pond, a second trail forks left, reaching Island Pond in 0.4 mile.

Long Pond, whose trout make it a fisherman's destination, has some high, dry shores, a fading path leading along the northwest, and a barely usable sunken rowboat. You could find a pleasant dry campsite on either the north or south shore.

Island Pond, however, is surrounded by swamps except one small southern portion a few hundred yards west of the end of the trail. Even its trail, which starts out dry enough as it leaves the Long Pond Trail to follow a natural ridge a little east of north, soon becomes very wet as it dips into a marsh area half way to the pond. You approach Island Pond through a bog, and without a boat it is difficult to appreciate its pine covered shores.

From late spring through fall, the walk to either pond makes a delightful nature exploration. In winter, the seldom used snowmobile trail makes a good intermediate ski touring route, but first you must ski in 1.8 miles from either direction along Padanarum Spur. Another approach to Island Pond is only good in winter. A snowmobile trail makes a tortuous trip almost following the line between private and public lands from the abandoned road south of Lily Pond, section 42. That trail was designed only by a desire to avoid private land. Its corkscrew route is cut so narrowly that only experts should ski along it. Snowshoers will find the route acceptable, and perhaps this is the best way to enjoy Island Pond, for winter is its best season.

Brant Lake

MODERN BRANT LAKE is a lovely resort with many good guest houses. The lake was originally called the Elbow, and its shores and the land along its outlet into the Schroon River were settled in the early 1800s. The old names for today's hamlets are a clue to the rich historical past. Horicon was known as Stickney's Mills, South Horicon was The Pitt, and a cluster of homes on the Schroon River near the confluence of Brant Creek was called the Tannery. Haysburg, Starbuckville, and Bartonville in the hills around Brant Lake were named after the farmers who pioneered those regions.

Settlers could clear productive farmland in the valleys, but the interior beckoned as a source of timber. A number of saw mills were built in the valley, and selected timbers were harvested from all the nearby mountains. Lumbermen in the Brant Lake area were the first to institute the Adirondack practice of sending single logs down narrow, twisted streams where logs could not be tied together into rafts and shipped in the traditional manner. From Brant Lake, the logs went into the Schroon River and ultimately to the mills at Glens Falls and Hudson Falls.

The tannery near Horicon was opened about 1840. Because of it and other industries, the town flourished from 1840 to 1880, during which time the population grew to exceed 1600. Horicon, like other Adirondack towns, began to shrink as the valuable forests that spurred its industry were depleted. It gradually declined to half its peak population, and maintained that low level until the 1950s.

42 Lily Pond

Hiking, camping, fishing, snowshoeing, cross-country skiing
2.3 miles, 1 hour, 380-foot elevation change

There are two accesses to Lily Pond, both 2.3 miles long and both have limitations. Lily Pond, however, is a very handsome lake with camping opportunities, and it is the only access today to four other remote and delightful interior ponds.

Grassville Road heads south from the shore of Brant Lake on NY 8 just 0.6 mile east of Duell Hill Road, section 40, or a little over 3.1 miles east of Northway Exit 25. The road once lead to the farming community of Grassville where sheep, buckwheat, and oats were raised. Now it leads into the wilderness. It climbs for a mile to a sharp bend that is usually plowed wide in winter to serve as a snowmobile trailhead. At the bend an old tote road heads due east, then north, then east again. Avoid a left fork, north, that leads to private lands at 1 mile. You stay straight, east, and reach state land at 1.2 miles. In another 0.4 mile, near a brook crossing, the trail intersects a road coming in from the south. That road from the south has access only over private land, so continue straight.

The tote road, edged with the stone fences of old farm fields, continues east through a gradually improving woods for 0.7 mile to a campsite on the southeast corner of Lily Pond.

The 2.3 miles from the parking area can be walked or skied in an hour. A hundred years ago a half dozen farm sites lined the road. Near the lake, the scrub forests of returning fields are punctuated by a few significant pine trees, but it is otherwise not a very exciting walk. The narrow trail heading south about 200 yards short of Lily Pond is the snowmobile trail to Island Pond, section 41. It is marked with a red disk and a large number 1.

The state recently acquired a tract of land that provides a second access to Lily Pond, this one from the north. It is along a dirt road, still used by vehicles but only marginally suitable for driving. Although extensive repairs were made to the road in 1980, you should not attempt the road without a high wheel base car. The road will remain a seasonal use access, closed in winter except to snowmobiles.

The road is a south fork from NY 8, 5.6 miles east of the Horicon Fire Station, at the point the highway leaves the eastern shore of Brant Lake and within sight of the bridge over Lily Pond Brook.

The first 200 yards passes through private land, and there is no parking near the beginning of the road. This makes it very difficult for those who wish to hike, not drive, to the lake. The road is fairly steep at the start and has a noticeable climb almost all the way to the pond. It crosses Lily Pond Brook three times on the way, each time on a bridge. A few large pines mark the otherwise small second-growth forest.

You should spot a few of the yellow DEC snowmobile trail markers along the route. Beyond the first bridge, at 1.3 miles, the road passes through tall grassy areas with alders and cedar. Near the second bridge at 1.6 miles the stream is quite handsome with rocks and fast water. Just beyond the second bridge there is a good parking area. At 1.9 miles, the road forks. The way right leads to the west side of the outlet. You can walk this section, but it is in very poor condition for driving. Just beyond, on the left fork, you reach the third bridge with a marsh and an old beaver dam visible upstream. You head gently downhill and reach the pond's northern shore at 2.3 miles. There is a reasonably good camping area on the north shore.

A yellow marked trail leads 0.4 mile around the pond's eastern end to the lovely campsite on the southeast corner. The yellow trail's intersection with the trail that connects Lily's south shore with Round Pond is unmarked. The south shore campsite is 100 yards west of the trail intersection.

This northern approach to Lily Pond is fairly steep for skiers and a hefty walk for those who do not drive backwoods roads. The camping destination is a worthy one, if only for the lovely view northwest to the cliffs on Sand Beach Mountain on the shore of Brant Lake. They appear to peep above the far end of the pond when viewed from the campsite. If you do drive, you can easily bring a canoe. But the best reason to reach the pond is to gain access to the trails that follow, leading to more and more remote interior ponds.

43 Round and Duck Ponds

Camping, hiking, skiing, fishing
1.4 miles from Lily Pond, 45 minutes, minimal elevation change

Round Pond is 1.4 miles east of Lily Pond along a dirt road now designated as a snowmobile trail. Round Pond is a gem, a delightful destination, but the dirt road approach is still used by four-wheel-drive vehicles that tear up the tread and spoil it for the hiker. Walking along it might make you think that it would be enterprising to own a beer concession at the trailhead, for mountains of cans have been tossed along the way.

Shortly after leaving Lily Pond's southeastern shore campsite, the trail circles east and crosses a small stream, then passes the yellow-marked trail that forks to the pond's northern shore. It then continues east with red markers through a grove of old apple trees, past stone foundations, and in less than ten minutes reaches a second intersection. Here the trail to Buttermilk Pond, section 44, forks left, and the way east leads to Round Pond in exactly 1 mile. The road is a disaster of mud and ruts, and a misleading V only leads to a bypass newly forced by vehicles. The descent to the pond ends at a delightful campsite on a high, dry, hemlock covered shoreline. Round Pond's reputation for trout explains the vehicles and the number of campsites along its western shore, each signaled by a rock ledge descending cleanly to water level.

Map VI: Sections 39-44

Based on USGS 15' Bolton Landing Quadrangle

A trail marked with 1 on a large red disk heads left, west, then north along the western shore. The trail actually forks in a wet seep at the north end of the pond, but the fork is obliterated. The right branch curves through the swamp, but is only obvious on the far shore where it continues north to intersect the trail to Buttermilk Pond. The red-marked snowmobile trail intersects the Buttermilk Pond Trail in 0.6 mile, offering the possibility for a loop walk.

The left branch is a narrow footpath climbing a small rise to a knoll covered with huge pine trees. You follow it through a beautiful cedar swamp and reach Duck Pond after little more than a five minute walk past Round Pond. Duck Pond boasts an aluminum boat, ducks, and a shoreline whose naked cedars tell of beaver flooding.

A second, unmarked path leads from the campsite at the end of the trail on Round Pond, around the east to the northern shore. A ten minute walk in this direction brings you to a pine covered campsite on a rock ledge that is bordered with trailing arbutus and pink lady's slippers. A spring walk to enjoy these flowers coincides with the height of the fishing season when vehicles are being used to reach the pond. Summer or fall would be better for walking. And a winter cross-country ski trip from Lily Pond would be suitable for intermediate skiers as long as they realize the minimum winter distance for the round trip to the pond is 7.4 miles, since the trek includes a round trip to Lily Pond.

44 Buttermilk Pond

Hiking, fishing, camping, cross-country skiing
3 miles from Lily Pond, 1½ hours, 300-foot elevation change

Buttermilk is the prettiest and least accessible of the interior ponds south of Brant Lake. Without a boat you might have trouble reaching a suitable campsite along its shores, but the long walk to reach it is also among the area's best.

From Lily Pond's southeastern campsite, head east as for Round Pond, walking less than ten minutes to the second, yellow-marked trail and turn north on it. The trail climbs gently and follows an old road that was so well improved it can withstand and give little evidence of the vehicles that use the first 0.6 mile. For that 0.6 mile, the road is bordered by stone fences, apple trees, and scrub forests that tell of farmland returning to forest. The old farm's front yard maples are the only large trees you will see.

The entire area north and east of Lily Pond was swept by fire in 1907.

The road, still bordered with stone fences, levels out and contours at grade on a fairly straight course north-northeast. The route begins to descend and is so easy it will only take half an hour to walk the 1.4 miles to another farm site where apple trees and a stone slab over an intermittent stream signal its past settlement. You cross to another ridge, turn east, and continue downhill, with steeper grades falling off to the left of the trail. Birch and small pine mark this pretty area where a few charred pine stumps tell of older forests. The needle littered trail makes wonderfully pleasant walking.

In this lovely section you should easily spot a large stone foundation close to the north side of the trail. This spot, at 1.7 miles, marks the easiest place to leave the trail for a short bushwhack detour, a little west of north, to Brindle Pond.

Continuing toward Buttermilk Pond on the trail, you walk for another ten minutes through lovely birch down to an open area where, at 2.2 miles, a special trout water sign near a stream crossing might make you wonder how the dried mud flat just downstream could ever hold trout.

On entering the woods again, you will find the wooden remains of a temporary structure. At this point the red-marked snowmobile trail, section 43, takes off to the right, south, for the 0.6 mile connection with Round Pond.

The trail to Buttermilk Pond suddenly narrows and becomes a footpath. It no longer follows a roadbed, but winds up a steep draw following an intermittent stream. The route is untouched, little used, and bordered with lovely ferns. You climb for about ten minutes to a height-of-land at 2.65 miles. The trail winds across the level, making a sharp bend to the left near a big double pine at 2.8 miles, about five minutes into the level walk. So few have come this way that the lack of foot tread makes you very dependent on the markers, and this could be a confusing spot, especially on the return. Just beyond the double pine, the trail begins to descend, and within five more minutes you catch sight of Buttermilk Pond.

Much of the shoreline is boggy, though there are several pretty rock ledges beneath tall pines. One huge pure white boulder on the far shore glares peculiarly in the sunlight, portraying perhaps the quartz whose outcrops have appeared in several places along the trail. Buttermilk Pond has the feel of a true Adirondack pond with its untouched shoreline and its remoteness from roads and people.

You can make the 3 mile return to the intersection east of Lily Pond in an hour, so with a rapid pace, Buttermilk Pond is about two and a half hours from either Grassville Road or NY 8 via the Lily Pond Brook Trail.

Generally the snowmobile trails in northern Warren County are getting far less use than a few years ago. The local ranger suggests that this trail and its loop to Round Pond are ideal for snowshoers who can make easy short cuts on the frozen ponds. Cross-country skiers, too, will find the roads ideal. Only the last 0.8 mile to Buttermilk Pond should be limited to expert wilderness skiers. You can substitute the fairly level 0.6 mile south to Round Pond and make a circuit back, section 43. Note this circuit follows a sometimes marshy course, making it unsuitable for summer travel.

45 Swede Mountain
0.5 mile, 15 minutes, 250-foot elevation change

All that remains of the trail to one of New York's abandoned fire tower sites is an unmarked path, and recent extensive logging has conspired to hide the path. The summit is nearly overgrown, and even most of the view is gone, though from late fall through early spring you may have glimpses northwest over the Pharaoh Lake Wilderness and beyond to the High Peaks.

To find the path, drive along NY 8 between Brant Lake and Hague, a beautiful trip in itself. The highway crosses a high mountain range, and views from the eastern slopes look across to Lake George's northeastern mountains. From the western slopes the view of the receding series of Adirondack foothills is equally impressive. A beaver flow north of the road just west of the height-of-land in the Joseph Dixon Memorial Forest is a good place for birds. North Pond is very narrow and stretches 0.6 mile along the height-of-land beside the south side of the highway. Parking turnouts invite you to stop and look for birds across its water.

At the far western end of North Pond, a small path leads from the parking turnout across a rickety bridge over the outlet, along the shore for 30 feet, and up into the woods. The footpath, which is filling in, leads to Swede Mountain. It headed west of south below a ledge, then south over it, and continued southwest along a narrow ridge to the tower site. With debris from logging concealing the path, you may find it easier to bushwhack on a compass reading of about 200° magnetic for the 0.5 mile trek to the summit.

Walk west for 200 feet from the tower site, then to the right about 20 feet, to find the rock outcrop with autumn views. When the leaves are off, you can easily pick out Gore Mountain a little south of west and Hoffman Mountain in the northwest, but there are no views to the south or east.

46 First Brother Mountain

Path, hiking, snowshoeing

A range of cliff-faced mountains tower above NY 8 east of Brant Lake. The three highest of these are First, Second, and Third Brother. The tops of Second and Third Brother have long been owned by the state, but the top of First Brother, with its spectacular views down the length of Brant Lake has until recently been privately owned. But now, the top of First Brother has been acquired by the state through the Nature Conservancy.

Turn north on Palisade Road from NY 8 at the east end of Brant Lake. Palisade Road crosses a marshy bay then ascends a little hill and starts a sweeping S curve. All along this portion the land has been posted— probably by landowners annoyed by inconsiderate people who leave messes on their land. Watch carefully as you come out of the curve back to the right about 1 mile from NY 8, and you will see a line of yellow paint blazes heading into the woods. These mark the beginning of state land and the next short, 0.2-mile, stretch along the road is marked with Forest Preserve signs. The shoulder is wide enough near the line to allow limited parking.

You can follow the blazed line, uphill, though it becomes too steep for snowshoeing. About 100 feet to the west is a faint path, visible only in summer, that leads up the mountain. You can either follow it or the blazed line. The latter is easier to follow on a snowshoe climb. No matter the time of year, you will be amazed at the number of deer that seem to like this wild hilltop.

You head up steeply through an evergreen woods for 100 feet or so, then the grade becomes easier and you can work back right to the blazed line. It is easy going following the paint blazes until you come to a place where the next blazed tree is up a ten-foot-outcrop. Again work to the left along a sort of ramp that takes you to the blazes on top the outcrop.

Next you will come to a thirty-foot steep cliff. Ahead is another knob on the chain, perhaps a "Little Sister" to the brothers. In summer you can climb directly over the Little Sister, but in winter the hardest part of climbing First Brother is getting around Little Sister. Going to the north involves a steep climb, but it is through evergreens so thick they will keep you from sliding off the sidehill. If you go around to the south, you cross onto private land. You traverse just below, to the right of, the steepest part, and find there is a 400-foot stretch with a near cliff on the right and a only a narrow sidehill throughway.

As you round Little Sister, your view across the little valley shows First Brother to be all steep rock face. Work back to the blazed line, which

will give you the best route. It leads you across a ridge overgrown with
dense saplings (push through). Turn left up an easy grade to the top of
the ridge of First Brother. Angling right you find you are on a not too
old logging road (the land was logged not long before the state acquired it).

Walk to the right, southeast for the best view. Continue to the summit,
which is wooded, and again you need to walk right, this time descending
about 100 feet to the top of a cliff with views south toward Catamount,
section 38, with Sugarloaf, east of Lake George, on the left, and Black
Mountain on the right.

Lumbering slash has left the top of the ridge and summit an unattractive
mess, and this does detract from the views. However, the forest will recover and the cliffs are so high that views will persist even as the forest
recovers.

Two hours suffice for the 700-foot climb and return in summer. The route
is steep enough that a snowshoe trek takes considerably longer.

47 The Brother Mountains
Bushwhack, hiking

The recent acquisition of First Brother Mountain creates the opportunity
for a six-hour traverse from east to west that covers the summits of all three
Brother Mountains. Leave a car on Palisades Road, section 46, for the end
of the trip and drive east on NY 8 to where Spuytenduivel Brook crosses
the highway, at the line dividing the towns of Horicon and Hague. An
old road comes out of the woods at this point. Though overgrown, it can
be your guide for the first part of this bushwhack.

The road is on high ground to the east of the stream and is easy to follow as it parallels the stream. After about 0.25 mile, the road crosses to
the west bank to avoid a very steep high valley wall on the east. From
here, the old road stays on the west bank and is sometimes obvious, sometimes either wet or overgrown. When in doubt, just follow the brook.

At about 1 mile in, you come to a swamp with open water held back
by a beaver dam. A steep bank on the left drops almost to the marsh,
which is a beautiful destination all by itself. This opening provides a lovely
view of the Barton Mountains. The one on the left with two humps and
a lot of cliffs is labeled Barton Mountain on the Graphite USGS map.
Also, a higher mountain behind Brace Mountain is labeled Barton Mountain, on the Silver Bay map. Between them are two small mountains with
very spectacular cliffs but no name. In this guide, the group is referred
to as the Bartons.

Skirt the left shore of the marsh at the bottom of the steep bank and you soon, within 0.2 mile, see an outcropping of rock to your left. In winter and wet times a small stream tumbles down the cliffs. Beyond this point you come to some tumbled boulders, with one very large one. Another 100 feet beyond the largest boulder is a good place to begin to climb the mountain, moving back toward the west and toward the little stream and the open rocks. Continue climbing along the steep valley wall. You may find the intermittent stream, which you can follow up as a valley forms around it. Finding this valley may save you from a lot more of the steep areas. The wall of this side valley will get higher as you go upstream and then starts getting lower. By climbing it to the left, you will get on the main ridge of the mountain leading to the summit from the east. The farther up the side valley you go before turning left, the easier your climb will be.

These cautions apply mostly to winter snowshoe trips. In summer you can more easily pick your way from open patch to open patch, eating blueberries as you go. Then it takes three-quarters of an hour to reach the beaver dam, about one and a half hours to reach the cliff tops at the southwest end of Third Brother Mountain.

As you ascend, you will see more open rocks ahead and each opening gives another wonderful view of the rocks and cliffs across the swamp to the Bartons. There are views south to Black Mountain and the Lake George region. Finally you will see the wooded summit and almost a sidewalk of open rock leading on a level course around to the western edge where you can look down at the lake and the road. From here there is an enticing view of No. 8, Little Stevens, and Stevens mountains. You can also see the open rocks on the ridge that lead from the Third to the Second Brother.

At this point you have three options: return the way you came, drop into the col, heading directly south following the valley until it levels, then swing to the east and quickly find yourself back on the Spuytenduivel about 0.3 mile from the road, or continue on to Second Brother. Note that the second option can be very tricky, as it is possible to get into areas where further descent is too steep and returning is more than difficult.

For the through trek, continue around the western end of the summit of the Third Brother, which becomes wooded close to the edge of state land. It is steep but very easy to descend to the col, which is full of white birches. Here you will find new yellow paint blazes marking the property line. Using the blazes as a guide, it is easy to work your way out to the open rocks along the ridge toward the Second Brother. There are also signs (some blazes, some plastic ribbons) of an old trail that leads to these rocks and also to the summit of Second Brother. (In summer, it takes an hour and a quarter to hike from Third to the summit of Second Brother Mountain.) The summit is wooded and unspectacular, but go directly west from the summit, descending about 400 feet, and you should find yourself crossing a small brook flowing north out of a boggy area.

As you leave the col between the First and Second Brothers, you will at first visually head for the summit, but you can also be guided by a line of old boundary blazes. But, you will soon find evidence of recent logging to the north, and you will be more attracted to the openings in the woods to your left, which will lead you to more spectacular views from open rocks on the south face of First Brother. (In summer, it takes an hour and a quarter to hike from Second to First Brother Mountain.) You can easily reach the summit, which is wooded and drops sharply at its western end, but you may want to stay to the south of the summit where the views are spectacular. Farther west, and lower, there is a false summit, Little Sister, section 46, with more wonderful open rock. This is the place that is so easy to reach from Palisades Road. The path down to the road will probably be easy to spot from here, although, to avoid private property, you should leave the path part way down and head west directly to the road. (In summer, the descent from First Brother takes about an hour and a quarter.)

48 Barton High Cliffs

Snowshoe bushwhack

If you climb Third Brother and look to the east, you will be impressed with the cliffs that range across the northwest slopes of two unnamed summits between higher peaks to the north and south, both called Barton Mountain. It is little wonder few know these cliffs, as they are not visible except from other bushwhack destinations. Even though you look down the length of Brant Lake from one perch on top the cliffs, you cannot distinguish the cliffs from the lake. They are behind a series of rugged mountains all of which have cliffy faces.

What a wonderful discovery you can make if you snowshoe to these little known cliffs that range for over a quarter of a mile along the unnamed mountain, designated only by its elevation 1910 feet. And so spectacular are they, that it seems appropriate to call them Barton High Cliffs.

The cliffs rise to almost 400 feet at their western edge and very few people know of their existence. A bushwack route to the top of the cliffs is sufficiently difficult that it is better done in winter to take advantage of greater visibility through the trees.

View of Third Brother from Barton High Cliffs

Drive east of Brant Lake, beyond Spuytenduivel Brook, and beyond a parking turnout on the left, north. East of that, you will notice that the road begins a wide bend to the right, and there is a large rock cut and a slide on the left. Turn around in a second parking turnout, on the right, on the hill. (This turnout has a lovely view.) Return to park just west of the open rock area at the end of the roadside barriers.

At this point, head north, up the steep grade, picking up a small stream that drains toward the highway. Rock ledges line the hill to the west. Follow the west side of the stream for a quarter mile, climbing 200 feet on the way. At the top, the stream turns east, going to the right of a little rocky knob; you continue north to the left of the knob and come out in a handsome, little hemlock grove. It occupies a draw between a shoulder of Brace Mountain and the lower slopes of Barton Mountain. Walk north for nearly 0.3 mile through the grove, heading northwest briefly to the left side of the draw. You pick up a small stream that develops in the draw and drains to the north. You descend from the col for about 250 yards, staying on the left side of the developing stream, until you reach a stream coming in from the northeast. Near this junction, cross over the stream you have been following to take up the stream flowing from the northeast as your guide. You climb slightly, cross a property line, and begin to climb more steeply.

As the stream swings to the east, your steep climb appears almost stopped as you enter a cirque with sharp walls all around. The stream tumbles over a small waterfall on your right, another, smaller, and definitely intermittent stream joins it just below the waterfall. Use that as a guide to climb out of the cirque, heading northeast again. This route levels out into a draw—on your right are the northwest slopes of Barton Mountain, on your left is the top of the unnamed hill with the cliffs. Notice that the hill is ringed with spruce covered ledges and cliffs. These and the real cliffs make climbing this hill from any other direction just about impossible. Continue following the draw, curving north. At the height-of-land, head northwest across the northeastern slopes of the unnamed hill. From here you can see Wintergreen Lake and Marsh through the trees to the north.

You have covered nearly three quarters of a mile beyond the stream junction. Do not be tempted to head south, uphill, across the top of the unnamed hill, looking for cliffs—that is not where the exciting ones are. Instead, drop down the northern, shallowest part of the ledges on the north slopes of the hill, cross a draw that is clearly defined on the 7.5' USGS map, and climb slightly to emerge on the top of the cliffs.

Barton High Cliffs

Watch your footing, but do walk both northeast and southwest to enjoy all the view. Below the cliffs lies a talus filled valley. Opposite is another unnamed hill with open rock patches, see section 49. To the west, you can see Second and Third Brother, and from a southwest point, you can look down Brant Lake and even see Pharaoh Mountain peeking up from behind the northern Barton Mountain.

The total bushwhack is about two miles. In winter, it will take between two and two and a half hours to climb, just short of two hours for the return. In summer, the bushwhack can be shorter, provided you watch your compass directions and carefully follow the outlined streams and valleys.

49 The Talus Caves and the Unnamed Hill
Bushwhack

If the trip to the cliffs sparked your thirst for discovery, you may want to climb the unnamed hill north of them for a vantage from which to view them. You also may want to explore the caves in the talus below the cliffs.

Follow the roadway along Spuytenduivel Brook, section 47, until it peters out at the foot, outlet end, of the marshy area, where a beaver dam holds back the upstream ponded water. It is best to cross the creek here, just below the dam, but this may present considerable difficulty in high water. The eastern shore is not marshy, follow it northeast to a beautiful, flat, open wooded area, possibly a good campsite. Then head almost due east to pick up a stream that drains the valley to the east of Brace Mountain. (This stream is flowing north; it curves west through the marshes and joins the outlet of Springhill Pond, which has become Spuytenduivel Brook.)

Following it upstream, will head briefly east, then south, for nearly half a mile. At this point you can begin to climb northeast up the unnamed hill that faces the cliffs. The lower slopes are surprisingly steep, cliffy enough to foil winter snowshoeing. There is a series of open patches along its southern and southwestern slopes, some quite low. You do not have to climb far for a look at the cliffs. And from these open patches, you can plan the best route to the area below the cliffs where the talus jumble resembles Indian Pass.

An earlier edition of this guide speculated on the location of the ice caves, known to nineteenth century visitors to Graphite. Robert Carroll, Jr., wrote of his exploration of this area; he is convinced that the talus jumble at the foot of Barton High Cliffs contains the legendary ice caves, but much more remains to be discovered.

Hague and Graphite

NY 8 PASSES through a small community called Graphite where the road descends east from the height-of-land at North Pond toward Hague on the shores of Lake George. The 1887 discovery of graphite, or *plumbago* as it was then called, quickly changed the surrounding country. Mines were opened by men who toiled at blasting and shoveling the hillsides for 10c an hour. Teams pulled sleds loaded with ore to a mill at Ticonderoga, and loads as large as four and a half tons went down the road toward Hague. By 1891 a mill, 100 feet wide by 500 feet long and five stories high, was built in Graphite to process the ore. Woodburning furnaces powered the engines that crushed the ore, consuming 10 cords of logs four feet long a day in the process.

Tunnels were pushed into the surrounding mountains. One mine was opened on the hill opposite North Pond, but the realignment of NY 8 closed its opening and obliterated all trace of it.

Slurry from the separation process was washed into Hague Brook, the lovely stream that NY 8 follows downhill to Lake George. Pollution became so terrible and protests so loud that a settling pond was built by damming the marsh where Wintergreen Pond now stands.

Ore was taken from open pits and from many miles of tunnels under the settlement of Graphite. All operations ceased in 1921, and most of the mines have collapsed. The mine area remains in private hands, but you can see the opening of one pit if you explore the south side of the road 0.2 mile east of North Pond. Look for a rock painted to emphasize its elephantine profile. Immediately west of this point, an abandoned roadway leads within 100 yards to several pit openings. The openings were blasted shut because they were such a hazard, but it would still be possible to fall into some, so walk carefully. In summer, you can feel cold, clammy air rising from them. Below ground, there were more than a mile and a half of passages, many now filled with water.

One of the nearby hills was called Big Notch and a famous ice gorge lay below its 300- to 400-foot cliffs. The gorge, a favorite hike for Graphite residents and recorded in their reminiscences, may very well be the talus caves below Barton High Cliffs, sections 48 and 49.

There are three trails whose origins are near Hague and Graphite, all good walks; but, unfortunately, none lead to points of interest from the mining days.

50 Jabe Pond

Hiking, camping, canoeing, fishing
1 mile, ½ hour, 250-foot elevation change

Jabe Pond is among the state's newer acquisitions. Provisions for its management will continue to permit motorized access, at least for the present, to a parking area 300 feet from the pond. The road is, however, steep, washed out, and almost unsuitable even for four-wheel-drive vehicles. It is gated during the mud season. At present the state plans no further road maintenance, so definitely consider this a walk.

Jabe Pond is best when viewed from the water, so it is desirable to have a canoe or inflatable boat. There are eight official campsites, and campers may select other sites as long as they are at least 150 feet from water.

Not only is Jabe Pond Road in poor condition, but access roads to it can also be very poor in early spring. The shortest and best is Split Rock Road, which turns west from NY 9N halfway between Silver Bay and Hague. The fork to Jabe Pond is 1.8 miles up Split Rock Road, and there is a parking area at the intersection.

From the parking area, Jabe Pond Road heads briefly downhill, then up through a scrub forest where the road is lined with pad leaf orchids in summer and a good variety of wildflowers in spring. Halfway through the walk the grade appears too steep for those who choose to drive. The road then levels out in a beautiful hemlock forest that takes you all the way to the pond.

The small view of convoluted shoreline that you have from the road end at the outlet of the pond gives you little clue to the wonderful bays and islands that beckon the canoeist. There is a campsite on the island in the south end of the pond. Jabe has been well stocked in the past and has something of a reputation with trout fishermen. Steep mountains frame it, providing many lovely vistas from handsome points along the shore.

A road heads southeast along Jabe's western shore. It quickly ducks back from shoreline, heading toward an old hunting camp but not before it crosses the outlet stream from Little Jabe Pond. On the south side of that small stream there is a fishermen's unmarked path that leads up another hundred feet in elevation in 0.3 mile to Little Jabe Pond, a tiny teardrop dwarfed by Indian Mountain.

Canoe campers and fishermen will certainly enjoy the larger pond. Hiking opportunities are limited, and trash has often been a problem here, especially at the end of the road. But the distant campsites that surround Jabe beckon all who enjoy camping.

51 Berrymill Pond

Hiking, camping, snowshoeing, fishing
3.1 miles, 1½ hours, 720-foot elevation change

The trailhead is north of Graphite and most easily reached from NY 8. Turn north from NY 8 to Summit Drive, 2.4 miles east of North Pond or 3 miles west of the intersection of NY 8 and 9N at Hague. (The latter road passes the very handsome falls on Trout Brook.) Drive west, then north on Summit drive, watching for the intersection on the right, east, with West Hague Road. Continue straight on the northern spur of West Hague Road. The trailhead is 0.7 mile north of the intersection.

The trail approaches Berrymill Pond from the southeast and connects with a trail from Putnam Pond, section 87. Warm water fish and two lean-tos are the main attraction of this pond, most of whose shores are swampy and low. The blue-marked trail begins by heading northwest on a jeep road, and three forest roads fork left, south, from it before the wilderness barrier is reached at 0.3 mile.

The trail, now only a footpath, angles to the north, fording a stream and passing the apple orchard of an old farm on the right. You cross a boulder wall at 0.5 mile and continue on a gentle uphill walk until at 0.8 mile the trail becomes much steeper as it enters a handsome white birch forest. Here it climbs the 400-foot ridge that forms a long continuous arc curving around the east side of Ellis Mountain and Burnt Ridge.

You cross a stream 1 mile from the trailhead, sometimes finding the stream flowing through the trail, and continue fairly steeply until a height-of-land is reached at 1.3 miles. You descend slightly through maples and hemlock and at 1.7 miles the descent quickens.

You cross a log bridge over a stream flowing toward Berrymill Pond at 1.75 miles. The height-of-land or the ridge marks the divide between the watershed of Trout Pond and Putnam Pond. Deep, wet woods of spruce, balsam, hemlock, and maple border the trail to the next stream crossing, a log bridge over a moss-filled brook at 1.9 miles. You cross another log bridge at 2.2 miles and continue walking through yellow birch to reach the inlet and cross it on a plank bridge at 2.65 miles. There is a good spring 250 yards beyond, and at just over 3 miles, a trail intersection.

The way right, a blue trail, leads to one lean-to, and in 2.1 miles to Putnam Pond State Campground. The way left, also marked blue, leads to the shoreline, and in 0.15 mile to a second lean-to.

The pond is nearly filled with waterlilies and water plants. If the lean-tos are filled, you will find an excellent camping spot on the rock penin-

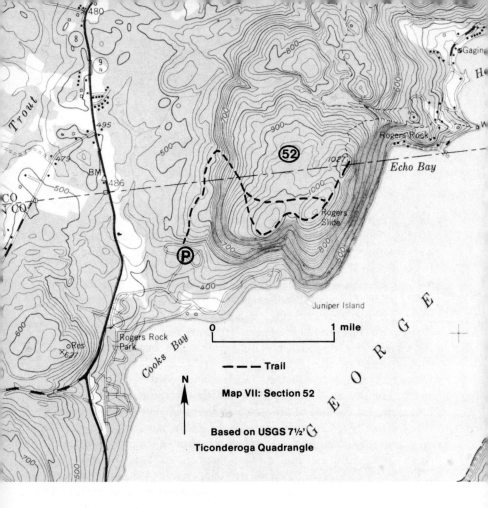

Map VII: Section 52

Based on USGS 7½' Ticonderoga Quadrangle

sula just west of the second lean-to. Beyond the first, the northern lean-to, which overlooks the small bay cut off from the main pond by the peninsula, you will find an even smaller bay. The outlet flows from it into a steep ravine, and you might enjoy walking down the outlet away from the trail to discover its waterfall.

Note that a trail also starting from West Hague Road once led to Springhill Ponds, which are also reached from Pharaoh Lake, section 60. The eastern end of the trail is on private land, but the Unit Management Plan soon to be adopted calls for 1.5 miles of new trail which will lead from a point near the beginning of the Berrymill Trail in an arc around the private land and connect with the old Springhill Trail. This will open the possibility of a through loop from Pharaoh Lake to Springhill to West Hague Road.

52 Rogers Rock

Hiking, scenic vistas
1.25 miles, 1 hour, 500-foot elevation change

Rogers Rock State Park straddles NY 9N, 3.5 miles north of Hague and 6 miles south of NY 74 at Ticonderoga. The park has excellent camping, swimming, picnicking, and boating facilities, and a great trail to the scene of a famous skirmish of the French and Indian War.

There is a day-use fee in summer months for the park. Rangers at the entrance can direct you to the trailhead. A faint blue daub on a tree opposite campsite #181 indicates the footpath. For the first 0.4 mile, you walk generally north and uphill, emerging from the woods below a rock ledge. A faint path leads on a scramble, straight up the ledge, climbing hand over foot. Within five minutes the vista begins to open up to the west.

The knoll that greets you after the 0.2 mile ascent is mostly open rock. You may spot a fork in the path at the beginning of the open rock; the way is not well marked and you can go either way. If you go left, across the open rock of the summit area, you cross one swale with wild iris and bristly sarsaparilla, then cross a second rock patch to emerge at an intersection on the cliff tops. The view is south beyond Anthony's Nose, past two bays on the west shore of Lake George whose curving shoreline points to Black Mountain on the east shore. The trail north, or right, stays close to the cliff top with continuous views, then dips back into the woods. It descends steeply over wooded ledges before heading out to cliff tops again, this time for the final drop down to the top of Rogers Slide.

The view from the slide itself is along the northern reaches of the lake, with Anthony's Nose blocking distant views south—an historic perspective. In March of 1758, Major Robert Rogers led 180 of his Rangers from Fort Edward on a scouting party toward Ticonderoga. Walking in deep snow between Trout Brook and Bald Mountain (now Roger's Rock), his men intercepted a party of about a hundred Indians. According to Loescher's *History of Rogers Rangers*, Rogers' men "scalped about forty Indians in about one quarter of an hour." The French, aware of Rogers' approach to Fort Carillon, set out to intercept the Rangers, bringing with them three hundred men, many of whom were Indians fueled with brandy and incensed at Rogers' scalping party. Rogers drew up his forces on the northwest flanks of the mountain and withstood two vicious assaults before ordering his outnumbered men to "disperse, and everyone take a different route to the place of rendezvous," where they had left their sleds on Lake George.

View Northeast from Rogers Rock

Rogers scaled Bald Mountain and crossed to the cliffs above the lake. At the spot of his now famous slide, he unlaced his snowshoes, putting them on backward, and backtracked away from the cliffs. He "swung himself by a convenient branch into a defile and followed it down to the lake." Indians, finding his tracks, marveled at his "escape" down the cliffs. But only fifty-two of Rogers' men survived this crushing defeat.

After pondering these sad events in our country's history, you can return by a slightly different route than your ascent. Wind back along the cliff top, up the wooded ledges and, in 0.4 mile, intersect the path across the summit. This time stay left, along the top of the highest cliffs. You enjoy a fantastic sequence of changing views from at least a half dozen places. You wind across the cliff tops for 0.4 mile, rejoining the summit path just before the plunge down the western face. Within fifteen minutes you return to level ground and, shortly after, the trailhead.

Pharaoh Lake Wilderness—the Southern Approach

THE PHARAOH LAKE Wilderness Area has the highest concentration of crystal clear lakes and ponds accessible from good hiking trails of any of the Adirondack regions. Each pond has a special character created by the varied waterfronts, rock ledges, and quiet coves, and each has a unique vista of mountains, cliffs, and wooded shorelines.

The mountains were all scraped by glaciers to produce their current shapes—long slopes to the northeast, sharp cliff faces on the southwest. The valleys are filled with glacial ponds and marshes, with dense forests pervading the generally sandy soil of the valleys.

It is not the effects of the glaciers that will seem most obvious to the hiker but the effects of forest fires. Dense pockets of hemlock and hardwoods fill unburned areas. Scrub trees and pioneering pine and birch struggle to survive on soil that has been burned repeatedly so that all organic materials have been consumed, leaving the earth infertile for many years. The entire summit of Pharaoh Mountain was burned, as was the area from Pharaoh Lake north to Treadway. The southeast shore of Pharaoh Lake was burned in 1911, and the effects of that fire are plain to see. Fire followed man, the loggers, and the tanbarkers.

The interior of the Pharaoh Lake Wilderness was settled only by lumber camps and the farms and boarding houses they spawned. Even as late as 1885, Pharaoh Lake was considered "an important body of water, surrounded by a group of dark and gloomy mountains. In this vicinity cluster numerous ponds, the fountainheads of valuable streams." This was no place to settle.

The pines, which the region produced in large number and unusual size on the glacial washes between the lakes, were all cut by the middle of the nineteenth century.

Several tanneries were built in the Schroon River Valley, a few of these before the Civil War. Canals and railroads had made it possible to bring hides from South and Central America and California to meet the country's growing need for shoe and boot leather. The traditional craftsman used vegetable materials for tanning and found the acres of hemlock in the Adirondacks rich in tannin. By 1850 the hemlocks of the Catskills and lower Hudson Valley were exhausted, and the tanneries moved north to be near the source. It was more economical to ship the hides to the wilderness than to bring the hemlock closer to either the source of hides or the shoe manufacturers.

At each Adirondack tannery, huge sheds, up to six hundred feet in length, were built to house rows of vats in which the hides were soaked in tannin extracted from hemlock. The soaking process took from six to eighteen months. A cord of bark when ground could tan only four hides. The tanneries were so large that some required yearly harvests of stacks of hemlock measuring eight feet wide by twelve feet tall and piled in series of sheds whose length totaled up to a mile and a quarter.

In the third quarter of the nineteenth century, two tanneries used hemlock from the interior of the Pharaoh Lake Wilderness. One was located in Millbrook, now Adirondack, at the confluence of Mill Brook and Schroon Lake; and a second, one of the Adirondack's larger operations, was on the side of the Schroon River just north of the confluence of Brant Lake Outlet. The latter, called the Horicon Tannery, depended on hemlock deep in the Pharaoh Lake Wilderness.

Hemlock was felled in early spring. The bark was stripped and carefully piled until the first snows. Then the piles were gathered, or "ranked" as it was called, on the sides of woods roads, so the ranks could be collected by teamsters who drove huge horse-drawn sleds into the wilderness as soon as the roads became frozen. When you walk the roads from Brant Lake to Pharaoh Lake, you follow the teamsters' route.

Perhaps you would like to muse on one of the teamsters, a woman with six small children, who daily set out into the woods with her youngest child, a fifteen-month-old baby in a wooden box insulated by pillows, at her side. In weather often twenty below zero they drove the length of "Brant Lake and on to Pharo."

53 Pharaoh Lake Trailhead, Beaver Pond Road and Pharaoh Road

The southern access to the Pharaoh Lake trails is tucked away at the end of a sequence of roads whose often missing signs may make finding the trailhead the equivalent of solving a mystery. Pharaoh Road is not plowed in winter, and driving over it the rest of the year can be difficult. Water often sits in deep pools and ruts in the roadway, and for a time in spring, the first quarter mile of trail north of the parking area at the end of Pharaoh Road is flooded. Something has to explain the fact that so many hikers and fishermen overcome these obstacles and manage to use the interior trails. That something is the rare beauty and wonderful series of camping spots along Pharaoh Lake and the numerous trails accessible from the shore trail.

To find the trailhead, drive east on NY 8 from Northway Exit 25, about 8 miles to Palisade Road at the head of Brant Lake. Palisade Road is 10.7 miles west of Hague and NY 9N. Turn north on Palisade Road and drive past Camp Road and Bent Lee Road, following Palisade Road as it curves around the northern bay of Brant Lake. Beaver Pond Road is a right, north, turn 1.6 miles from NY 8. Pharaoh Road is also a right, north, turn from Beaver Pond Road, 3.1 miles from NY 8.

Drive, walk, snowshoe, or ski the 1.4 miles from Beaver Pond Road to the parking area at the end of Pharaoh Road near Mill Brook. The trailhead was the homestead of the Culver family in the late 1800s. Their fields were the plowed lands around Mill Brook. In the 1930s a CCC reforestation project replanted the farm, creating the forests you see today.

Note that the Unit Management Plan calls for the trailhead to be moved south to the Wilderness boundary, and a barrier will be placed on Pharaoh Road, less than 0.5 mile from Beaver Pond Road. This closing will add 2 miles round trip to all the Pharaoh Lake trails.

Because the roadway is not plowed in winter, it has become a very popular ski route. The parking is at Beaver Pond Road where a good-sized swath is kept plowed, accommodating six to eight cars. From Beaver Pond Road to the parking area plus the Mill Brook trek, section 54, is a novice ski trail. From the parking lot to the lake, section 55, is more challenging but not difficult.

54 Mill Brook
Snowshoeing, cross-country skiing

As you travel the road to Pharaoh Lake trailhead from Beaver Pond Road, you pass the junction with the old Mill Brook Trail that parallels Mill Brook. If you are walking or snowshoeing, the junction is about a fifteen minute walk past the third of the three summer camps along the road. Look for the place where you first enter the cathedral-like grove of white pines. Just as you reach these, you will see an opening to the left, leading

slightly downhill into a messy blowdown, where trees have been toppled by the wind. Also visible, about 30 feet from the road is a DEC Wilderness Area sign.

What appears to be an old tote road disappears in undergrowth and blowdown. However, if you investigate and persevere, after crossing a small stream, you will find the way opens up and becomes quite clear even though there are no trail markers and very few blazes.

The trail parallels Mill Brook, which is visible a good share of the time through mixed forest. At one point about ten minutes from the road, there is a nice view of Pharaoh Mountain as you pass a broad marshy section of the brook. The trail is relatively flat and straight, making a pleasant ski or snowshoe trip for about 2.6 miles. As it begins to climb slightly, you will notice that there is more undergrowth. Soon you see yellow paint blazes and a posted sign marking the beginning of private property.

You can return the way you came or drop down along the property line to the edge of the brook. Here you will see signs of recent beaver activity. The brook bank has little undergrowth and is quite level, so that, especially if you are on snowshoes, it is easy to explore as you head back toward Pharaoh Road. You can continue along the brook bank or easily return to the trail at almost any point. There are some nice boulders along the brook, occasional views of open rocky areas on No 6 Hill to the north and Pine and Orange hills to the northwest. Some spots along the brook would make nice picnic stops.

55 Pharaoh Lake

Hiking, camping, fishing, cross-country skiing, snowshoeing, canoeing
2.45 miles, 1 hour, 215-foot elevation change

The trail to Pharaoh Lake from the Pharaoh Road parking area follows a road that was used by vehicles until the area was designated a Wilderness in 1972. It is designated for hikers and horsemen, but the beginning is unmarked and you will find very few of the blue disks that are supposed to denote the trail.

Immediately north of the parking area, the trail crosses Mill Brook on a plank bridge, continues north through the wet meadow that often floods the trail, and heads up the Pharaoh Lake Brook Valley in a pine reforesta-

Mill Brook

tion area. Other old logging roads, all unmarked, do intersect the trail, but even those unfamiliar with the route should have no trouble staying on the correct course. At the first intersection stay right.

A gentle uphill followed by a relatively level trek describes the first thirty minutes of walking to a trail juncture. Here, at 1.15 miles, a detour left takes you to a good camping spot on an evergreen covered promontory, high and dry above the wide flow and marshes of Pharaoh Lake Brook. In winter skiers often travel this far and explore the marshes before returning. The best part of the detour is the view, north, across the marsh to the sharp cliffs on the steepest face of Pharaoh Mountain.

The right fork, the continuing trail, turns east to cross Pharaoh Lake Brook. The trail turns northeast beside the flow, then climbs away from it. A second flow comes into view on the left at 2.1 miles. The trail stays straight at the next intersection 0.2 mile farther. The marked trail intersection with the Sucker Brook-Desolate Brook Horse Trail is at 2.4 miles, and the trail junction at the outlet of Pharaoh Lake is less than 100 yards beyond. West of the outlet you will find a spring on the beginning of the West Shore Trail. It is near the site of a logging camp that later served hunters and fishermen.

The lovely ledges that face the narrow southern arm of the lake are only a taste of what is to come. The continuing trails, the one following the old roadway on the west shore or the yellow trail on the east, will take you almost all the way around the two-mile-long lake. Pharaoh is among the larger lakes with a shoreline that is entirely state owned. You almost ought to have a boat or canoe or inflatable craft to explore the myriad coves and bays. The access trail is so wide and smooth that you would have no trouble pushing a canoe on a bicycle-wheel cart.

The wide and relatively level trail has a second advantage. It is ideal for cross-country skiing, and skiing is a great way to explore the lake shore. While the trail is suitable for novices, note that your route trip to the lake in winter is 7.7 miles because of the unplowed road. Even beginning to see a part of the lake makes this at least a 10-mile outing.

56 Pharaoh Lake, the West Shore Trail

Hiking, fishing, camping, swimming
1.6 miles, 1 hour, minimal elevation change

Head west across the bridge over Pharaoh Lake Brook at the outlet of Pharaoh Lake. The trail has both red and yellow markers. In 0.1 mile there is a spring. You pass the side trail to the first of three lean-tos at 0.4 mile. The trail right, east, leads in 0.1 mile to a lean-to on the shore. The trail north splits again at 0.75 mile, with the yellow spur leading right, northeast, 0.3 mile to two lean-tos on a gorgeous pine and hemlock-covered peninsula. The more northern lean-to sits atop a rock ledge that drops cleanly to water level. Both lean-tos are handsomely sited and are beautiful places to camp.

The red trail, left, continues north through hemlocks around a marsh and crosses a small stream at 0.95 mile at the head of a deep bay. The trail stays back from the shoreline for the next 0.25 mile, where it crosses another small brook. At 1.6 miles the trail turns west-northwest, away from the lake, leading to Pharaoh Mountain, section 57. A spur leads 100 feet to shoreline, where a sign directs boaters to this trailhead for the Pharaoh Mountain Trail. No trail continues northeast to the head of the lake to intersect the east shore trail. However, a 0.6 mile bushwhack between the two, along the shoreline, takes only a half hour, section 58. The Unit Management Plan calls for the construction of a trail along this shoreline, although there is no scheduled date for its completion.

57 Pharaoh Mountain from the Southeast

Hiking, distant views
1.55 miles from Pharaoh Lake, 2 hours, 1400-foot elevation change

From the lakeshore trailhead on the western shore of Pharaoh Lake, section 56, walk 100 feet to intersect the main red trail. The way northwest begins with a moderate uphill for 0.25 mile to the base of a 100-foot rock ledge. The trail becomes steep as it curves north around the ledge, finally resuming a more westerly course. You are climbing the north side of the long southeastern shoulder of Pharaoh Mountain, where the trail rises 500 feet in 0.3 mile through predominantly hardwood forests. Near the crest

of the shoulder the way is steep, but here for 0.1 mile the trail passes through stands of evergreens.

The trail levels somewhat at 0.8 mile, continuing across the top of the shoulder to reach bare rock at 1 mile. Already you can enjoy good views to the east. In the next 0.25 mile the trail climbs moderately through hardwoods. At 1.1 miles you begin the steep ascent of Pharaoh's summit knob, reaching a lookout at 1.4 miles. In the last 0.15 mile you cross the summit, walking on rock ledges to discover a variety of views, including a delightful one southeast to Pharaoh Lake. The tower stands on open rock, and the best views northwest are from ledges near the tower. You have to walk north following an informal path between open rock patches to reach lookouts to the northeast.

58 East Shore of Pharaoh Lake

Hiking, camping, swimming, fishing
3.9 miles, 2½ hours, minimal elevation change

From the Pharaoh Lake Outlet, a yellow trail leads northeast along the eastern shore. The route, partially in woods, is most often so close to the shoreline that there are an infinite number of tree-framed views of Pharaoh Lake, its mountain, and of Treadway Mountain. The trail winds north beyond an intersection with the trail from Putnam Pond, sections 88 and 89, and Wintergreen Point, to a northern corner of the lake, 3.5 miles distant, where the trail to Crane Pond, section 72, heads north, uphill. With a detour to Wintergreen Point, which is 0.2 mile long, a 7.4 mile round trip walk from Pharaoh Lake Outlet will take at least 5 hours, not because of the difficult walking, but because of the number of stops to enjoy the views, the shoreline, or to swim. Still, the distance is not too great for a 12.3-mile day hike from the Pharaoh Lake Trailhead. An interesting alternative is the 11 mile circular walk around the lake with this trail, a short 0.6 mile bushwhack, and the west shore trail. If you were skiing to the lake, you would probably use the frozen lake surface rather than the trail, but you would certainly want to duck into each of the tiny bays along the way.

From the outlet of Pharaoh Lake at the unmarked intersection with the west shore trail, walk east past the field that was once the front yard of the ranger's cabin. From the field there are lovely views of the long rock-edged finger of the southern end of Pharaoh Lake. A horse trail forks right, uphill, but quickly rejoins the main trail.

The trail crosses a wooded hillside, back from the shoreline, and passes a horse barn at 0.4 mile. It is slated for removal. Beyond there are two small lean-tos with views across to Pharaoh's islands.

Just beyond the lean-tos, at 0.5 mile you should notice a yellow marked trail heading through the hemlock forests to Whortleberry Pond. Treadway Mountain and its ledges are visible to the north-northeast. You continue along the old roadway, on bare rock, between patches of blueberries. This area was badly burned in the fires of 1911 and little topsoil remains.

At 0.7 mile you pass a third lean-to, and 0.1 mile farther there is a fork in the trail. The way east is the red trail to Springhill Ponds. Continue on the left fork, where you cross a plank bridge over a brook in 100 feet and a plank bridge to a peninsula 200 feet farther along. At 0.9 mile you reach the fourth lean-to, this one situated beautifully on the end of a long thin rock peninsula. This lean-to has a sand beach, some of the best swimming in the lake, and views of Treadway and a part of Pharaoh Mountain, just visible to the northwest. You will meet many similar ledges in the Pharaoh region, most, but not all, trending north-northeast to south-southwest. All were created by glacial scraping and grinding. The long, rounded ridges with fairly steep sides are called *roche moutonne*, sheep backs. The rock ledges are repeated in the lake, forming little islands in front of the lean-to; they are fun to swim to.

Cross the long, thin bay back to the shoreline trail on a narrow log bridge and continue walking northeast on the yellow trail. In the next 0.7 mile you walk close to shore, enjoying some of the best views of the entire walk. You can see the cliffs on Pharaoh Mountain beyond the lean-to promontory on the west shore.

You cross more of the *roche moutonne*, then the going gets a bit rougher. A steep hillside with ledges drops to shoreline, forcing the trail over boulders and through narrow clefts. The trail looks as if it were seldom used. You may walk this far before you find the first of the yellow markers that are supposed to designate the trail.

The rugged tumble of boulders drops to shoreline, and the hillside is covered with a few really big hemlocks. At 1.7 miles, more than an hour's walk along the lake, you approach a ledge covered with red pine framing views of Pharaoh Mountain. A double yellow marker alerts you to a sharp right turn; if you continue 100 yards north you are opposite Wintergreen Point, so close you feel you can touch it. The trail circles east around Wintergreen Bay, and you have to walk 0.8 mile just to reach the point that seems so close.

On the circuit, the trail continues high on an evergreen covered ledge winding over boulders and outcrops. You look across Wintergreen Point and Bay to Pharaoh Mountain. There is a giant old beaver house in the waterlily-filled bay. At the north end of the bay, you see the inlet stream that flows from Wolf Pond and Devil's Washdish, high on the side of Treadway. The view from the bridge of waterfalls on the stream is especially lovely. Just beyond, at 2.3 miles, you reach a trail intersection of all yellow trails. The right fork leads in 3.25 miles to Grizzle Ocean, section 88, and the left fork leads 0.2 mile to Wintergreen Point.

In summer a detour to the point for a swim is almost mandatory. It is a lovely secluded spot, and there is a campsite at the base of the peninsula.

The main trail, straight ahead, now swings west of north, up on a pine and hemlock covered ridge that is so dense there is almost no undergrowth and the foot tread is concealed in deep needle cover. The place has a noble beauty; it is one of the most beautiful of the deep, dark woods for which the Pharaoh Lake Wilderness is best known.

At 2.8 miles the trail swings close to a small bay, then heads up through a second deeply shrouded promontory. The yellow trail markers are definitely needed to follow the trail, which emerges on the shore of Split Rock Bay at a lean-to with the most wonderful views of all.

As you continue north along the shore of the bay, the trail becomes quite wet, and blowdowns and a swampy area may force you to improvise your route. There is a spring at the head of the bay. Beyond it the trail swings west, then south to follow the shoreline. A huge split rock looms up in the bay, surrounded by smaller boulders artistically placed by the glacier. The small bay provides a reflecting pool for the sculptural mass, softening the contours with reflected light and the tracery of pickerel weed and twisted stumps.

The best place to view the rocks is from a spot far out on the side of the western arm of the bay. The trail crosses that western point, and in 0.1 mile reaches the turn north to Crane Pond, section 72, and the end of the east shore trail.

59 Whortleberry Pond
0.3 mile from Pharaoh Lake, 10 minutes, minimal elevation change

The yellow trail to Whortleberry Pond leaves the shore of Pharaoh Lake 0.5 mile from the outlet intersection. It heads almost due south along a

kame covered with stately hemlock. A kame is a hill or short ridge of strati-fied glacial drift formed at the edge of the glacial ice. Material transported by the ice is deposited by water flowing from the ice to form the kame.

The short route through the handsome open forest is scarcely a foot-path. It approaches the pond on the northwest side of a swamp.

If you continue on the west side of the water, you have to walk along a narrow footpath in such dense evergreens that it is almost impossible to stand up straight. There are several campsites around the pond; the best sites are on the southeastern shore, and a path of sorts circles the lake. Consider the trip around the pond a bushwhack. It is nearly 2 miles long because the informal path ducks away from shoreline at several points in order to avoid the marshes. If you like nature treks, this one is worthwhile.

60 Springhill Ponds

Hiking, camping, fishing, horseback riding, cross-country skiing
4.4 miles from Pharaoh Lake, 2½ hours, 650-foot elevation change

This long trail, originally designated for horse travel, will become a foot trail when the Unit Management Plan is adopted. The trail begins at the shore of Pharaoh Lake and circles around the southern shoulder of Thun-derbolt Mountain to approach Springhill Ponds from the south. The trail-head at Pharaoh Lake is 0.8 mile from the outlet intersection, or 3.25 miles from the Pharaoh Lake Trailhead. A shorter approach from West Hague Road is now closed, though a new route, see section 51, will be constructed. Then Springhill Ponds will be accessible from both east and west, but cur-rently they must be considered either a camping destination or a long round trip walk from a camp at Pharaoh Lake.

The trail is marked with yellow disks as it leaves Pharaoh Lake, headed slightly north of east. In 40 yards you cross a small brook and begin to climb to a draw between two small hills. At 0.6 mile you are at the height-of-land of the draw, a small ravine with moss covered boulders and a brook running its length. A slight and gradual descent follows, bearing east and crossing a little brook at 1.05 miles. You descend into a small depression, then up to a forest of white pines and hemlock, reaching a swampy area

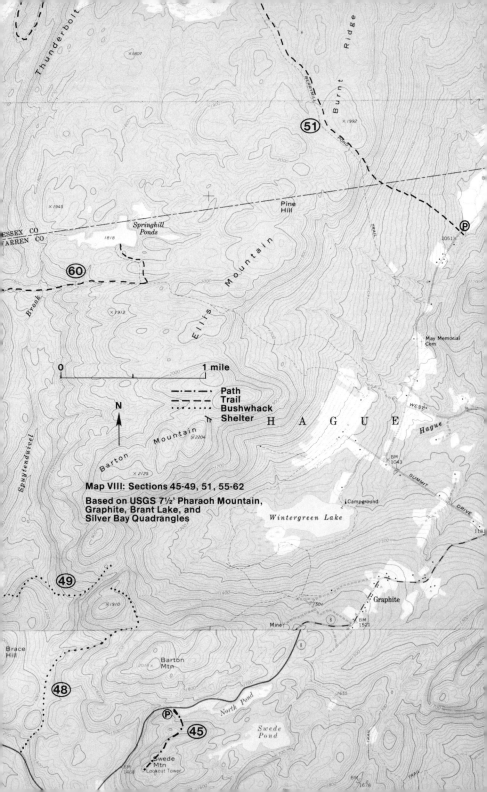

Thunderbolt

Burnt Ridge

×1807

BURNTHILL POND

⑤1

×1992

Pine
Hill

×1945

ESSEX CO
WARREN CO

Springhill
Ponds

1818

⑥0

Brook

×1912

Ellis Mountain

TRAIL

Ⓟ
1051×

May Memorial
Cem

0   1 mile

- ·- ·- Path
- - - Trail
· · · · · Bushwhack
⋀ Shelter

N

Mountain

§2204

Barton

×2125

Map VIII: Sections 45-49, 51, 55-62
Based on USGS 7½' Pharaoh Mountain,
Graphite, Brant Lake, and
Silver Bay Quadrangles

H A G U E

WEST

Hague

BM
1043

SUMMIT

DRIVE

118

Campground

Wintergreen Lake

⑭9

×1910

Graphite

8

BM
1521

Spuytenduivel

Brace
Hill

⑭8

Barton
Mtn

2018

Mine

North Pond

8

7655

Ⓟ

⑭5

Swede
Pond

Swede
Mtn
Lookout Tower

BM
1468

BM
1678

TRAIL

at 1.2 miles. A second brook, this one flowing from south to north, is reached at 1.3 miles.

A short rise at 1.9 miles leads to a sharp right-angle turn in the trail, which now heads south. You pass a swamp on your left, a ridge covered with hemlock and birch, and then at 2.35 miles cross a brook flowing north. The trail now gradually curves to resume an easterly direction, rising through a draw that marks the end of Thunderbolt Mountain. Beyond the height-of-land, at 2.9 miles, you may spot the remnants of a hunting camp. You continue east and cross the outlet of Springhill Ponds, Spuytenduivel Brook, at 3.1 miles. There are falls and a deep pool in a second tributary of Spuytenduivel Brook, which you reach at 3.4 miles. You climb sharply beyond the stream and cross still a third tributary at 3.6 miles. The trail stays close to this intermittent stream and crosses it again before reaching, at 3.9 miles, an intersection. The way straight ahead leads to West Hague Road. The way left, north, leads in 0.4 to the southern shore of Springhill Ponds.

At 1818 feet in elevation, Springhill is supposed to have good trout fishing. The trail is rarely used by horsemen and is quite delightful for hiking. Its grades give the trail an intermediate cross-country ski rating.

The trail toward the West Hague Road is still marked with red disks for almost 1 mile east to a barrier that marks private land. The barrier, placed at the end of private land on a jeep road, is 1.3 miles from West Hague Road. Public access has been granted in the past, but no easement has been given. Hence, a new trail will be built from the Berrymill Ponds Trailhead, section 51. If you are interested in the possibilities of a through walk, or a shorter approach to Springhill Ponds, check the status of this trail with the DEC Warrensburg office.

61 No. 8 Mountain
Bushwhack

If you look north across the very northern spit of Brant Lake, you can see a handsome mountain with an inviting perch on top, a rock ledge slightly below and to the left of the summit. This intriguing mountain with an elevation of 1850 feet has a rather nondescript name, No. 8 Mountain. As further assurance that the first surveyors ran out of names, there are hills designated as No. 6 Hill, No. 7 Hill, and No. 8 Hill, all just north of No. 8 Mountain.

You will find it is a fairly easy bushwhack to the outlook, a climb of 900 feet. Start by driving or walking north on Pharaoh Lake Road exactly

1 mile from Beaver Pond Road. This is short of the present Pharaoh Lake Trailhead by 0.4 mile, but well past the line dividing state and private lands. Take a compass reading of 127° magnetic, 112° east of true north, and follow it faithfully. For the first 0.25 mile you are on the floor of the valley, and there are little wet places and hummocks. You have to get around or over these, while still maintaining your compass course. The last 0.75 mile is up an easy slope through relatively open woods. If you follow the course precisely, you will come out slightly below and southwest of the summit. If you seem to miss the place and err by walking too far north, which would lead you over the summit, turn southwest to correct the course.

There are actually two flat ledges, one above the other, with a fairly steep rock and grass slope between them. From either of these lookouts, there is a fine view down Brant Lake to Crane Mountain and beyond. Particularly from the upper lookout, the view of the lake and rugged mountains is a striking contrast to the very attractive and manicured Bent Lee Farm at the foot of the mountain. The climb up should take about an hour.

62 Pharaoh Lake via the Sucker Brook-Desolate Brook Trail

Hiking, cross-country skiing
7.4 miles, 3 hours, 800-foot elevation change

When spring flooding makes crossing Mill Brook flow too difficult, you can find an alternate route to Pharaoh Lake. It is a much longer approach, but a very interesting hike, and as the local ranger says, much more suitable for hikers than for horses. The trail is a good wilderness cross-country ski route with an expert rating. With a car at Beaver Pond Road and another at the Blair Road Trailhead, you have a superior ski loop of 11.25 miles.

To find the trailhead, drive due east from Adirondack on the shore of Schroon Lake for 0.7 mile to an intersection. Turn north for 0.4 mile to Blair Road Trailhead. If you are planning a through ski trip, you can reach the Beaver Pond trailhead by turning south at the intersection onto Johnson Road. Johnson Road intersects Beaver Road in 1.75 miles where a left, east, turn leads to Pharaoh Road. The signs for these roads have been missing at times in the past. In fact, the area has a reputation for missing road signs as well as missing trail signs.

The trail begins as an old woods road that once led to farmhouses in an old settlement known as Gregoryville. You can see old foundations, stone walls, and signs of abandoned farmlands, all along the road, all dating to the early part of the nineteenth century. The fields are now stately pine plantations.

Bushwhackers will be intrigued to know that to the east of the trail there is a small, sharp little mountain with cliffs. You have to bushwhack to reach the tops of the cliffs, which lie less than 0.5 mile east of the trail and over 500 feet above it, but you will be rewarded with views of Schroon Lake and the Schroon River Valley and surrounding mountains.

The route of the trail begins a gentle uphill through mixed forests. You cross a small brook at 0.9 mile; near a second, 0.1 mile farther, you can see two old house foundations.

At 1.5 miles the trail angles right, to the east, away from a marsh beside Sucker Brook. The trail climbs slightly in the valley of Sucker Brook and follows that valley for 2.5 miles, rising only 440 feet in that distance. At 2.5 miles the trail passes a large marsh that normally has a resident beaver. Here the old road ends, and the trail, now narrower, continues up a short grade to cross a small brook at 2.7 miles. The forest is more open, of older, more mature hardwoods. You continue climbing gently and then, after a short and steadier climb, reach the height-of-land or saddle between Sucker and Desolate brooks at 4 miles.

In 0.2 mile you pass an open area with level exposed rocks, shallow soil, and many signs of deer browse. Now the trail begins to descend fairly rapidly, dropping 400 feet to the level of Desolate Brook in 0.6 mile. The trail is level near the brook, passing through stands of balsam, black spruce, and hemlock. You cross Desolate Brook at 5 miles.

In the valley, the trail turns north to follow the brook for 0.5 mile, through mostly coniferous forests. The valley of Desolate Brook all the way north to Desolate Swamp, northwest of Pharaoh Mountain, was rich in hemlock and heavily cut for tanbark. At 5.5 miles the trail again turns, this time to the east, to cross a hill that is a southern extension of Pharaoh Mountain. The 200-foot climb is easy, and you reach a large boulder that marks the height-of-land at 6 miles. The trail winds across the hill for nearly 1 mile, crossing several small streams. At 7 miles the trail descends steeply to the south, again following an old logging road. Signs of farmland are again visible. You walk within 50 feet of Pharaoh Lake Spring, and 0.1 mile farther, at 7.4 miles, you cross Pharaoh Brook to join the trail from Mill Brook and the south.

The hike from Blair Road to the lake will take the better part of 3 hours, even though the way is fairly easy.

East Shore Schroon Lake

AN EIGHT-MILE-long dirt road runs parallel to the east shore of Schroon Lake. At the southern end the road passes many summer camps, but farther north the road swings way east around Steep Bay Hill, so that it is quite close to a string of interior ponds in the Pharaoh Lake Wilderness Area.

The southern end of the road existed early in the 1800s, as did Alder Meadow and Crane Pond roads in the north. The through road was not built until this century. Today it is considered one of the Adirondacks' scenic drives.

From the south and Northway Exit 26, head briefly north on NY 9, going through Pottersville, and turn east on Adirondack Road just before the Word of Life sign. The road east takes you past a public access for boats and across a neck of Schroon Lake. Turn north, following the signs 4.4 miles to Adirondack. There, turn left past the Post Office on a road that quickly changes its name from Red Wine Road to East Shore Road.

From the north and Northway Exit 28, head south on NY 9 for 0.6 mile to Alder Meadow Road and follow it east for 2.1 miles until it splits. The left fork is Crane Pond Road, the right is East Shore Schroon Lake Road.

There is limited roadside parking at all the trailheads along the road.

63 Spectacle Pond

Hiking, camping, fishing, cross-country skiing
1.6 miles, 1 hour, 360-foot elevation change

Spectacle Pond is a good fishing pond stocked with trout and also a delightful camping destination, but its most attractive feature is the view east across its marshes to the cliff face of Pharaoh Mountain. The walk to the pond is as handsome as you could wish, for the entire distance the trail follows Spectacle Brook in its 360-foot drop from the pond.

The marked trailhead is 5.8 miles north of the Post Office at Adirondack. In the last 0.5 mile before the trailhead, East Shore Road pulls away from Schroon Lake, following Spectacle Brook.

Map IX: Sections 47, 53-59, 61-64
Based on USGS 7½' Pharaoh Mountain
and Graphite Quadrangles

Trail
Path
Bushwhack
Jeep Road
Road
Shelter

0   1 mile

N

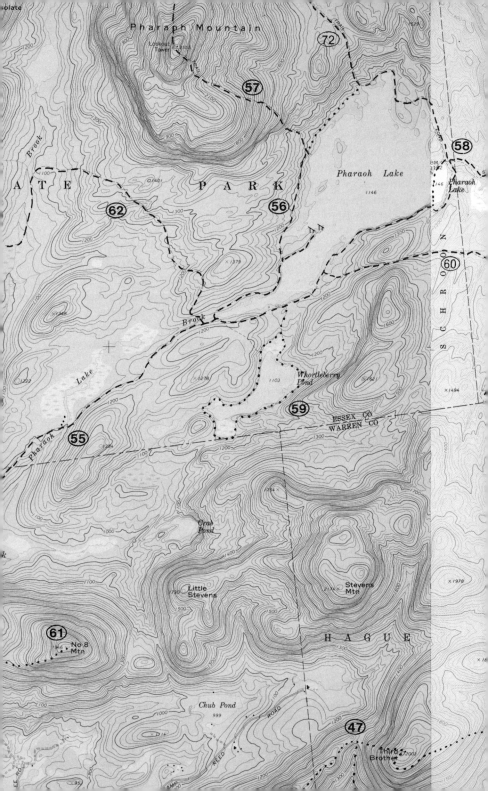

The trail follows an old tote road to the pond, and the roadway makes a wide, easy walking trail. It begins, marked with yellow disks, climbing a short rise to cross Spectacle Brook in 150 yards. You walk on the south side of the stream for a time, passing a lovely small waterfall. At 0.2 mile, you recross the brook. The forest cover is small, but a good rich understory of blooming spring plants and the dripping moss ledges, pools, and slides in the brook make pleasant company.

At 0.5 mile the brook splits and the trail crosses the left branch, the outlet of Harrison Marsh, near the confluence. The trail continues gently uphill beside the brook. A sense of deep woods pervades in spite of the small forest cover. The dense hemlock forest shuts out all other trees and gives the woods an open park-like appearance, as pretty as any in this wilderness.

At 0.7 mile the trail is close to small rapids and a pool in the steep ravine that holds the brook. Oxalis and crinkleroot carpet the forest floor. Beyond, the trail becomes rockier as it rises to the level of the pond. Big birch are here filling the hemlock forest. At 1.1 miles, you can already see the pond.

Your approach is to the broad marshes that border the outlet and over which you have that great view of Pharaoh Mountain's cliffs.

The trail continues southeast over a little rise and down to the outlet at 1.2 miles. You have to hop rocks to cross the outlet. Pause here to enjoy the arched trees and their reflections that frame the double view of Pharaoh. A man-made flood dam for logging at the outlet has been repaired by beaver.

The trail crosses to high ground of an esker and continues along the south shore. Just beyond the outlet there is a neat little camping promontory between the trail and the pond. You drop down to pond level again and reach the official end of the trail at a campsite 1.6 miles from the trailhead. You will find a fire ring and a small stream nearby. An informal hunters' path continues around the shore on the right, then climbs the hill to the south. The only boats found at the pond did not seem seaworthy, but a boat or canoe would definitely enhance a fishing or camping trip.

The roadway to the marsh is wide enough to make a good intermediate wilderness cross-country ski route. A circle around the frozen marshes of the pond extends this to a 5 mile trek.

64 Harrison Marsh

Hiking, snowshoeing
1.1 miles, ½ hour, 290-foot elevation change

An informal path, flagged with red ribbons and red and white paint daubs, leads 0.6 mile from the Spectacle Pond Trail to Harrison Marsh. Walk 0.5 mile along the Spectacle Pond Trail to the split in Spectacle Pond Brook. The northern tributary, the outlet of Harrison Marsh, has the delightful name Shanty Bottom Brook.

You should spot the path a few feet before the bridge over Shanty Bottom Brook. The path follows the west side of the brook most of the way to the marsh. The path crosses to the east side at 1 mile, just beyond a thick evergreen stand. You reach the rock spillway from the marsh at 1.1 miles.

Even though most of the shoreline is wet and filled with marsh plants and shrubs, you can find a small knoll between two beaver dams in the direction of magnetic north from the outlet. Here you will find a picnic spot and an excellent place to watch for water birds and ducks in the marsh.

65 Gull Pond

Hiking, fishing
0.5 mile, 15 minutes, minimal elevation change

Gull Pond is another of the stocked ponds in the Pharaoh Lake area with a good reputation for trout fishing. The much-used path to the pond is less than 0.5 mile, and the pond itself is only 0.25 mile long. You will find delightful picnicking beneath the tall pines that border the pond on the west. A thick carpet of pine needles covers the shore. You can easily circle around the pond, improvising your route, and climb the rock cliff that faces the unnamed hill west of the pond. From the cliff tops, there is a picturesque view of the entire pond.

The trailhead is 1.7 miles south of Alder Meadow Road and 6.8 miles north of Adirondack. The yellow marked trail heads southeast, passes through a wet area, then swings east to climb a height-of-land at 0.35 mile. A short descent brings you to the eastern shore of the pond.

Trail to Crane Pond from NY 74

66 Wilcox Pond

Nature walk
0.2 mile, 10 minutes, minimal elevation change

An unmarked, informal fisherman's path leads to Wilcox Pond. A dying body of water, now filling with marshlands, it offers an abundance of plant and animal life for the nature lover. From its shores are good views east to the north flank of Pharaoh and slightly north of east to sharp little Carey Hill.

The path begins 1.2 miles south of Alder Meadow Road. The foot tread is obvious enough to guide the hiker the short distance to the pond.

Northwest Corner of the Pharaoh Lake Wilderness

THE CRANE POND access to the Pharaoh Lake Wilderness Area is one of the most popular places in the Adirondacks. Treks to waterfront camping on a dozen ponds and the climb of the Wilderness area's highest peak all pass by Crane Pond. You can currently drive to Crane Pond, but proposals in the Unit Management Plan for the Pharaoh Lake Wilderness Area call for closing Crane Pond Road 1.9 miles from the pond. This may add a bit to each hike, but it will protect the beauty and fragility of this lovely area.

The road to Crane Pond is a very old one. Farmers settled the flats north of Schroon Lake in the first decades of the 1800s. In 1811, Charles Harrison began lumbering around Crane Pond and Pharaoh Lake. The region was covered with white pine more than ninety feet tall. Below them was a four-foot-thick layer of pine needles (duff) in which no vegetation grew.

Tyrell Road is named for a pioneering family, and Elihu Griswold farmed the nearby area called Alder Meadow. The rich forests of the wilderness to the east attracted many early lumbermen. In the 1830s, there were saw mills at Alder Meadow, Crane Pond, and Paradox Lake. When the Reed Lumber Company built a dam on Alder Brook, some of the Griswold's farmland was flooded, and Griswold sued for damages. Later, Crane Pond became the center of a large logging operation and boasted a "hotel," a typical boarding house, and a small settlement, a school, but no church.

Knapp and Faxon, Antwine, and Hiram Smith were other lumber companies in the vicinity of Crane Pond. Haskell, Farr, and Brandy lumbered there in 1876. Many of the small companies were bought up by the Raquette Falls Lumber Company, which still owned the land when it was sold to the state in 1908, the year of the region's biggest fire.

If the modern hiker does not find stumps to indicate the past logging, it becomes difficult to believe the area was logged at all. Forests of tall pine and hemlock alternate with mature hardwoods to cover the lower trails. Only on the steeper slopes are signs of logging really obvious, and there the clue is the fires that followed the loggers. Fires burned the organic topsoil down to bedrock. Open hillsides and ledges abound. These are the most attractive features of the wilderness.

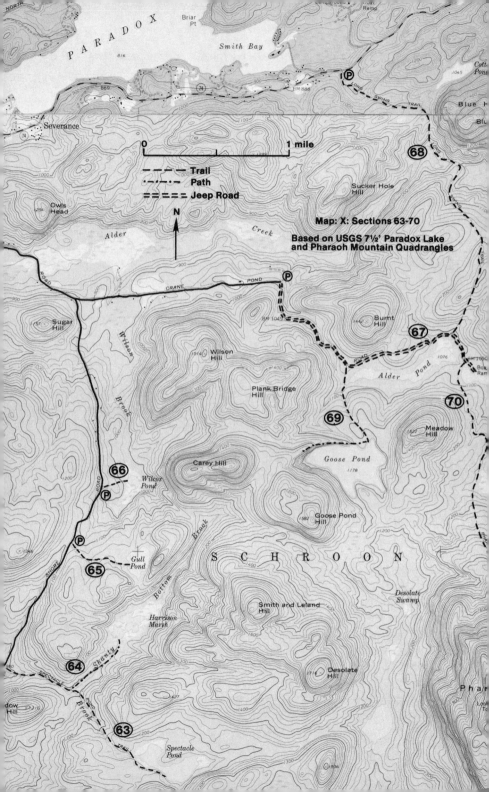

PARADOX

Briar Pt

Smith Bay

NORTH

Severance

Owls Head

Alder

Creek

0   1 mile

Trail
Path
Jeep Road

N

Map: X: Sections 63-70

**Based on USGS 7½' Paradox Lake
and Pharaoh Mountain Quadrangles**

Sucker Hole Hill

Blue H

Blu

68

CRANE   POND

67

Sugar Hill

Wilson Hill

Burnt Hill

Alder   Pond

Bor Ram

Plank Bridge Hill

70

69

Meadow Hill

Carey Hill

Goose Pond

66

Wilcox Pond

Goose Pond Hill

S C H R O O N

65

Gull Pond

Desolate Swamp

Harrison Marsh

Smith and Leland Hill

64

Desolate Hill

Phar

63

Spectacle Pond

67 Crane Pond from the West

Hiking, swimming, camping, fishing, cross-country skiing
1.9 miles from the new parking area, 45 minutes, 140-foot elevation
change

The new parking area for the Crane Pond Trailhead is 1.4 miles east on Crane Pond Road from its turnoff from Alder Meadow Road. The 1.9-mile walk to the pond is a handsome dirt road, great for walking or cross-country skiing.

From the parking area at the bend in the road, head south, uphill, following Alder Brook. The road has a gentle uphill grade, and, as it curves to the east, the falls on Alder Brook roar their presence. The deep, hemlock-covered gorge is very pretty. Near the head of the ravine the road again curves south, then turns sharply east to cross Alder Brook on a new bridge at 0.65 mile. At the next bend, 0.86 mile, the trail to Goose Pond, section 69, heads south.

The road now pulls away from the marshes on Alder Pond, going over a small hill. As you descend from the hill, in spring or wet periods, you will usually be chagrined to see the road flooded. Beaver work at Alder Pond keeps the marsh on the northeast corner flooded above road level. You can take your shoes off and wade or find a footpath around the swamps to the north. Some summers you may find no flooding at all.

On the east side of the swamp, at 1.6 miles, the Long Swing Trail forks left, north, to NY 74. This alternate access to Crane Pond is described in the next section.

At 1.85 miles the road ends in what was a huge parking area with wonderfully tall and stately pines. The trails south begin on the bridge and dam at the outlet of Crane Pond. There is a sign-in booth for hikers, so be sure to register if you are going on.

There are many lovely campsites around Crane Pond. Some are within 150 feet of water and camping will be restricted at some of these in the future. At all other places, here as elsewhere, camping is permitted as long as it is 150 feet from water.

Glistening birch make every bay a special place and the cliffs on Bear Mountain dominate Crane Pond's northeastern bays. For most, Crane is a jumping-off point to the interior, and with short walks from the outlet, a half dozen lean-tos and a number of campsites can be found on quieter and more secluded ponds. A canoe or boat certainly enhances a visit to the pond, and there is still some good fishing, though none of the twenty-five- to thirty-pound pickerel touted in an 1872 vacation guide.

68 Crane Pond from the North

Hiking, cross-country skiing
2.8 miles, 1¼ hours, 400-foot elevation change

You may find the Crane Pond access from the north preferable to the popular Crane Pond Road route. The walk is only 0.9 mile longer, and you rarely meet other hikers. Best of all, the walk is along a true wilderness trail through a forest of stately proportions.

The deep cool of the majestic trees covers the entire route. Huge pine, hemlock, and balsam fir overshadow the wide trail, leaving pine needles underfoot and making walking very easy on the carpeted floor. The dense evergreens crowd out new tree growth, so the woods take on a park-like and open appearance, almost as if the lower story of the forest had been cleared away. There are lovely vistas through the deep, hushed woods all along the trail.

A lush growth of ferns thrives in the filtered light on the forest floor. White birch have found a niche beneath the evergreens, brightening the dark forest. The trail circles the west side of Blue Hill, and that sharp little peak is visible through the trees for the first half of the walk.

The parking area is a turnout on the south side of NY 74, 4.1 miles east of NY 9, just 0.2 mile west of the entrance to the Paradox Lake Campsite.

The blue-marked trail climbs a bank, then parallels the road heading west to join an old tote road, heading east-southeast toward Blue Hill. You cross a small stream, the outlet of Cotters Pond at 0.15 mile, then continue gently uphill to recross the stream at 0.25 mile. A third log bridge crosses a smaller stream at 0.5 mile, and just beyond, the trail angles sharply right, south, to pass quite close to the cliffs and ledges of Blue Hill. You pass a height-of-land on the lower slopes of Blue Hill at 0.7 mile and descend to the level of a swamp at 1.2 miles. In the next 0.3 mile the trail has been rerouted away from the swamp, which has been enlarged by beaver activity. Beyond the swamp you begin to climb again, for a short time, fairly steeply. In 0.15 mile, the trail levels off again to skirt the east side of a second swamp with log bridges over wet areas.

At 1.8 miles the trail resumes a gentle uphill to a height-of-land at 2.3 miles. A long but gentle descent takes you in 0.25 mile to Crane Pond Road, 0.25 mile west of the outlet of the pond.

Junction Trail from NY 74 and Crane Pond Road

69 Goose Pond

Hiking, fishing, swimming, camping, cross-country skiing
0.6 mile from Crane Pond Road, 1.45 miles, forty-five minutes from
the new parking area, 220-foot elevation change

Goose Pond is heavily used by fishermen who find its trout waters quite rewarding. The yellow trail, only 0.6 mile long from the Crane Pond Road, see section 67, heads south with yellow markers from a point 0.85 mile east from the official parking area. At present you can drive directly to the trailhead, making it easy to carry a canoe to the lake for fishing or camping.

The trail immediately crosses the outlet of Alder Pond on a high plank bridge. The outlet of Goose Pond joins Alder Brook on your right, then the trail pulls away from the Goose Pond Outlet and begins a gentle ascent. Here, the trail is filled with rocks and roots and shows signs of heavy use. It can be very wet in spring, but log bridges take you over the worst of the wet spots. The trail levels at 0.4 mile and then descends slightly to a campsite on the lake shore.

To extend the walk, head west on an unmarked path beside the shore. It leads to several other good campsites and to a vantage on the western shore with tremendous views of Pharaoh Mountain across the pond. Afternoon sun delineates the cliffs and emphasizes Pharaoh's steep face.

The pond has delightful swimming as well as fishing. There are several aluminum boats at the pond; most, however, are secured. You would enjoy a canoe on the pond.

The trail is rated for novice skiers; a trek around the frozen borders of the lake is recommended.

70 Pharaoh Mountain

Hiking, views
2.8 miles from Crane Pond, 4.7 miles, 3 hours from the new parking
area, 1475-foot elevation change

Pharaoh Mountain with an elevation of 2556 feet is the tallest in this Wilderness Area. From every angle it is as conspicuous as the highest of the region's gneissic peaks. Cliffs face the fault block on the western slopes of this typical truncated cone. The views from its bare summit are spectacular. The fire tower on its summit still stands, though it is slated for removal in the future. The views are limitless even if you do not climb the tower.

The hike starts with the 1.9 mile walk to Crane Pond's outlet and mileages are given from there. Head south on the red-marked trail across the outlet of Crane Pond. The trail immediately plunges into a deep hemlock and pine forest. The needle-strewn route contours south around Meadow Hill to a trail intersection at 0.7 mile. The mountain trail is a right fork still marked with red. You cross a small brook and come so close to Glidden Marsh that you really should leave the trail for a view of Pharaoh Mountain and its reflection in the quiet waters of this long, thin pond.

At 0.9 mile you pass a picnic table and a good campsite situated not far from massive boulders and glacial erratics that lie beneath the tall trees. You begin a gentle ascent, and shortly the cover turns from deep evergreens to the smaller hardwood forests. At this point you have reached the limits of the fires that ravaged Pharaoh's summit.

As you continue up you notice a second route, the straighter course of the old tower telephone line. The red trail cuts back and forth across it several times on the climb.

At 1.5 miles, less than an hour's walk from Crane Pond, you notice you are climbing much more steeply. The trail is often on the smooth bedrock, the results of the fires burning most of the topsoil away. The climb continues steeply for 0.5 mile following a course toward the south. At 2 miles, a stream crosses the trail and often spills along it. You continue steeply on open rock with only scrub spruce and birch to shelter you from the wind.

There is a spring on the side of the trail at 2.6 miles, 0.2 mile from the summit, and even this may be dry. The end of the trail is very steep, with a 200-foot climb in a little more than 200 yards.

There are two rock outcrops on the long summit area. The tower sits on the southern outcrop, and a ranger's cabin, also slated for removal, is tucked in the cleft between the two.

Views from the south overlook Pharaoh Lake with Whortleberry Pond beyond. The distant mountains seen over the ponds are the ranges that border Lake George. You can easily make out the valleys of Lake George and Northwest Bay and identify the peaks of Black, Elephant, Erebus, and Buck Mountains on the east shore.

In the distant southwest beyond Schroon Lake Valley, you can see Crane Mountain twenty-four miles away, with Eleventh and Gore ranging to the west. Only a part of Schroon Lake's ten-mile length is visible. To the right of Gore you can spot Moxham Ridge, Blue Mountain on the distant north-

west, with Vanderwhacker over the northern end of Schroon Lake. Hoffman Mountain is the highest peak in the Blue Ridge Range that points north to the High Peaks.

Giant and Rocky Peak Ridge lie almost due north, with the High Peaks ranging west of the valley of NY 73. In order, to the left of the valley, you can name Dix, Macomb, Nippletop, Gothics, Saddleback, Basin, and the cones of Haystack, Marcy, and Skylight.

From the northern outcrop you overlook Treadway Mountain. The distinctive slide of Knob Hill is east of north. The panorama of the Green Mountains of Vermont fills the eastern horizon.

71 Crane Pond to Lilypad Lean-to, passing Glidden Marsh, Oxshoe, Crab, and Horseshoe Ponds

Hiking, camping, swimming, cross-country skiing
3.75 miles from Crane Pond, 2 hours, 200-foot elevation change

This portion of the trail DEC has designated the Short Swing Trail takes you past two lean-tos and a number of campsites near a variety of waterfronts. Whether you use this trail as a part of longer hikes or as an access to interior campsites, you will find it a good nature trail and a rich source of artistic views for your camera. Remember, however, to add nearly an hour and 2 miles to the trip to allow for the walk from the official trailhead to Crane Pond.

As you begin your walk through one of the most beautiful, deep forests of the Pharaoh Lake Wilderness, you will find it impossible to imagine what the trail you follow was like over 130 years ago. At that time there were four or five farmhouses along a rough road, approximately the course of the modern trail, in the 1.45 miles between Crane and Oxshoe ponds.

You begin on the red trail south of Crane Pond, walking 0.7 mile to the fork where the red Pharaoh Mountain Trail heads south. You take the blue trail southeast toward Glidden Marsh. The narrow blue trail leads you down to a stream with a bridge in 100 yards, through a hemlock valley to a small boggy marsh at 0.95 mile. Corduroy paves the way until you reach the shoreline of Glidden Marsh. At 1.1 mile, the blue trail forks left, uphill, away from the marsh.

Outlet Crane Pond

A sharp ascent of 120 feet in 0.1 mile takes you to high ground between Glidden Marsh and Oxshoe Pond. You wind across that high ground with little ups and downs to 1.35 miles where you begin a descent to Oxshoe Pond. At 1.45 miles you reach the Oxshoe Pond lean-to.

The view from the lean-to is across the east shore of the long pond to a magnificent rock ledge. The lean-to is on a ledge surmounted with giant white pine and a mix of red pine and birch. Lily pads float on the shallows, breaking the reflections of the enormous pine.

The trail, if you can pull yourself away, continues east through a thick hemlock grove that overlooks a swampy area to the north. Beaver have now dammed this swamp so that it is level and perhaps even a foot higher than Oxshoe Pond. A charming pine covered knoll borders the new pond. The trail begins a moderate climb to reach Crab Pond at 1.95 miles. Pretty white birch again accompany the trail as it begins to contour southeast around the shore of Crab Pond. The long thin ridges, *roche moutonne*, lie perpendicular to the trail, forcing you to walk up and down over several small hillocks. A footpath leads out into the lake on one of these to a rocky knoll with red and white pines, crunchy lichens and lady's slippers and a really great view of the sheer rock face of Pine Hill to the northeast.

At 2.1 miles, you reach the outlet of Crab Pond. Here a beaver dam has raised the water level 18 inches above the level of the natural rock dam. The outlet spills into a rock edged ravine made handsome with birch and pine. Less than 100 yards beyond there is a trail junction. The way right is the red trail, section 73. You continue straight beside the pond past pine-capped islands and promontories and another beaver house. Smooth rocks slope to water's edge where bays are filled with pond weeds. Blueberries and bunchberries fill the niches between the rock slabs on the shoreline.

Beyond a peninsula that is covered with hemlock so dense only a few birch can sprout beneath, you will find another tent site. At 2.5 miles, about half way along the 0.8 mile pond, there is a beaver dam on the left holding back a small brook that flows into Crab Pond. At this point, the trail winds along the top of terminal moraines that separate the pond from low and flooded land to the south.

Where the trail is near the shore there are fantastic views of cliffs and ledges on the north shore. Two beautiful rock ledges and a beaver house mark the ascent to a small peninsula that thrusts north into the pond. Giant pines and a few old stumps crown the promontory. Beyond, the blue trail hugs the shoreline with another series of wonderful views of the north

Outlet Crab Pond

shore and its ledges and huge rounded boulders. You reach the inlet at 2.75 miles, and cross it by hopping rocks.

The outlet of Horseshoe Pond plunges almost vertically to the level of Crab Pond, and the trail zigzags up for 80 yards on the east side of the outlet. At 2.8 miles you reach an intersection at the top of the ridge. Signs point left to Horseshoe Pond, where a five-minute walk along an unmarked path will take you to a lovely camping promontory in the center of the shore. Here a long flat rock thrusts into the water so the spot is surrounded on three sides by the pond, giving the pond the horseshoe shape.

The blue trail continues northeast across relatively level ground for 0.4 mile, though steep ledges drop from trail level on the right. You walk on one of these ledges around a small marsh and climb to a ledge, which has been bared by fire, at 3.3 miles. Here a sign points to the summits of Pharaoh and Treadway Mountain. Summer foliage hides them from view. Immediately beyond, the trail begins to descend, steeply at first, through a forest of fallen giant beech. Deadfalls and new growth make the trail difficult. The descent continues more moderately to a trail junction at 3.65 miles. Here the blue trail swings north toward Tubmill Marsh, section 74. In 0.1 mile you can walk east following a red trail across a small stream to the lean-to above Lilypad Pond. The lean-to, at 3.75 miles, sits on a red-pine-covered knoll overlooking the tiny, teardrop-shaped pond.

72 Pharaoh Lake from Crane Pond

Hiking, camping, cross-country skiing
3.45 miles, 1¾ hours, 340-foot elevation change

From the outlet of Crane Pond, follow the red trail 0.7 mile to the first intersection, then the blue trail 0.4 mile to the intersection on the side of Glidden Marsh, section 71. The northern shore of Pharaoh Lake is straight ahead on the yellow trail, 2.35 miles distant. This disagrees slightly with the guideboard at the intersection. The signs in this wilderness are not accurate, and part of the problem lies with the designations of the ends of the trails.

The first part of the yellow trail is the loveliest, passing Glidden Marsh, which is filled with water lilies. White pine on the far shore and white birch reflect in the marsh's dark water. You pass a little hemlock knoll that separates the trail from the water, then continue beside the marsh of cat tails, reeds, and cedar that fill the eastern end of the pond.

At 1.55 miles you leave the marsh, crossing the inlet on a slippery bridge. The trail begins the ascent around the east side of Pharaoh Mountain by plunging into a deep hemlock thicket. You should spot a giant spruce on the side of the trail, its 2-foot diameter making it one of the forest's larger specimens. A mature hardwood stand follows, its tall straight trees growing on Pharaoh's slopes. This is a true climax forest, a pocket of virgin hardwoods.

At 1.8 miles a trail forks left to Crab Pond. You continue climbing gently but steadily through a mixed forest of large maples and beech. Just before the trail levels off at 2.5 miles, the forest is predominantly beech, some of mammoth proportions, but all dying. Enough are dead already that new dense undergrowth of small trees has filled the forest floor and crowded the trail.

Beaver have recently dammed a small stream at 2.6 miles, forcing the trail to divert west around the flooded area. Here you will find two log bridges in need of repair. The trail continues relatively level near the stream, passing at 2.75 miles, a deep, wet swamp with standing water. All the Osmunda ferns are present, the royal, cinnamon, and interrupted. The algae-filled pool shines bright green against the dark green of moss and lichen-covered ledges and stumps that surround the pool. Again the size of the beech and hemlock covering the trail will astound you.

You pass a log bridge at 2.9 miles, and reach a height-of-land at 3.15 miles. The trail begins a descent, which quickens to a moderate grade. There are two rather steep sections, and from the second you can see the lake through the trees. You drop 300 feet in 0.3 mile. Pharaoh Lake is 65 feet higher than Crane Pond. From here you can walk east along the shore trail, section 58, or bushwhack 0.6 mile along the west shore to intercept the west shore trail, section 56.

The best way to make use of this trail is to combine it with a traverse of Pharaoh Mountain, sections 57 and 70, a short bushwhack, then this trail, walking it in the reverse direction to complete a loop of 8.4 miles from Crane Pond, 12.2 miles (8 hours) from the official trailhead.

Tubmill Marsh

73 Crab Pond from Pharaoh Lake-Crane Pond Trail

Hiking, camping, cross-country skiing
0.45 mile, ¼ hour, 80-foot elevation change

This short, 0.45 mile section of red trail takes you from the yellow Crane Pond-Pharaoh Lake Trail to the blue trail at Crab Pond. Use it to create a 4.4 mile loop from Crane Pond, passing Glidden Marsh, Crab and Oxshoe ponds. This circuit offers a fair sample of the ponds and forests of the Pharaoh Lake Wilderness. Three steep pitches in the trail make this an intermediate ski loop.

At the intersection 1.8 miles from Crane Pond, section 72, the blue trail forks left, northeast, and descends to a rock-hopping crossing of a small stream at 0.15 mile. Then the trail climbs steeply to a ridge through a mixed forest and reaches a flat open rock area at 0.35 mile. There is a three-way, all blue intersection at 0.44 mile. The way left, west, leads past Oxshoe Pond to Glidden Marsh, section 71, and the way right follows the shore of Crab Pond to Horseshoe and Lilypad ponds.

Mountains and Cliffs

THE NORTHERN PORTION of the Pharaoh Lake Wilderness has a cluster of small mountains with cliffs that are as inviting as the region's cluster of ponds. Each hilltop has a different range of views, and all are easy to reach, if you like to bushwhack. However, bushwhacking here is a relatively simple matter, and most of the great views are no more than a thirty-minute climb from a marked trail.

While the level trails are excellent cross-country ski routes, the bushwhacks are wonderful for snowshoe trips. The desirability of a bushwhack for snowshoeing is assumed throughout this chapter, and only mentioned on those mountains where there are special winter problems.

Fault scarps produced the jagged hills; glaciers and fires are responsible for the bare summits. All the hills have steep slopes, though not all in this group face the southwest. Vegetation is beginning to reclaim the fire-scarred and open rock summits, but the views will survive for several more decades. To top it off, these scrubby summits have acres of the best blueberries in the east.

The hills are accessible from Crane Pond or Putnam Pond, but the best and shortest approaches are from NY 74. One trail with two trailheads gives access to five superb little peaks.

74 The Old Tubmill Marsh Trail

Hiking, skiing, camping, snowshoeing
2.9 miles, 1½ hours, 400-foot elevation change

Take NY 74 east of Northway Exit 28 for 7.5 miles. Here there is a small parking lot on the south side of the road at the Ticonderoga town boundary. At 7.9 miles there is a larger turnout. A trailhead lies halfway between the two turnouts. The route south from the trailhead is to be abandoned and no more work will be done to improve it.

The first 0.1 mile of this blue trail is a disaster, as it crosses a wet, rocky field. The ferns, including maidenhair, and the cedar swamp are good, but the walking is not. Roots and rocks make a mess of the narrow footpath. You cross a log bridge at 0.1 mile and wind up a little hill to a plateau at 0.2 mile. You are traversing a mixed hardwood forest with birch, maple, basswood, beech, all tall and straight and interspersed with big white pine and red pine and hemlocks. This contrasts sharply with the logged area you skirt at 0.4 mile. The trail now follows an old logging road, and the woods are open enough to permit views of Ragged Mountain.

At 0.6 mile you meet a road that was once the main road west from Eagle Lake. The western part of the road is private land, but the way east is the access from the new trailhead. The continuing route to Tubmill Marsh is described in section 75.

75 The New Tubmill Marsh and Lilypad Pond Trail

Hiking, skiing, camping, snowshoeing
3.3 miles, 2 hours, 400-foot elevation change

A new parking area is being constructed at the outlet of Eagle Lake, 8.4 miles east of the Northway. This will be the principal trailhead for the routes to Tubmill Marsh and Lilypad Pond and south. It intersects the old route in 1 mile, but adds only 0.4 mile to the total walk and the northern portion is a much pleasanter walk. You will enjoy this trail as a walk to Tubmill Marsh, or as a means of reaching the best places from which to begin four of the mountain bushwhacks.

All mileages are given from this new trailhead, and the distances from it to interior locations are given in the following chart:

Destination	Mileage from New Trailhead
Tubmill Marsh	2.2
Lilypad Lean-to	3.1
Horseshoe Pond	4.05
Crab Pond	4.2
Oxshoe Lean-to	5.4
Crane Pond	6.85
Pharaoh Lake Lean-to	6.75

The trail, with blue markers, follows the old roadway, first crossing Paragon Brook, the outlet of Eagle Lake, on a good, new bridge. The trail then angles southwest, curves around the head of a marsh below Ragged Mountain, and continues west close to the base of Ragged Mountain to intersect the old Tubmill Marsh Trail at 1 mile.

The roadway takes a level course except for a long, gentle hill just past the bridge; the grade and width make this most desirable for cross-country skiers. The best part of the route is that it passes beneath the tall pines and hemlock for which the area is famous all the way from the highway to the Tubmill Marsh Trail.

At 1 mile, the trail turns south, left, following the traditional route, and makes a sharp descent of 50 yards to a spring at the foot of Ragged Mountain. You skirt a swamp that extends from Pyramid Lake to the slopes of Ragged Mountain and at 1.15 miles you cross a stream and begin a steady climb.

The ascent continues to a level at 1.5 miles, then resumes to a height-of-land at 1.8 miles. Note this spot, for it marks the place to turn off for the Bear Mountain, section 77, and Ragged Mountain, section 79, bushwhacks. The trailside is rich in ferns and unbelievably tall poplar trees. You cross the height-of-land for 0.1 mile, then begin to descend. At 1.95 miles there is an enigmatic sign labeled Potter Mtn., but pointed back along the trail. This is the point of departure for the Potter Mountain bushwhack, section 78.

The trail continues to be easy to walk. Halfway down the slope, at 2.1 miles, there is a red trail forking right, downhill, for 0.1 mile to a lean-to which is situated back from the shore of Tubmill Marsh, but not far enough back to avoid the insects that plague the marsh in early summer. Ignore the insects and explore the shore for views and reflections. A stump forest fills the marsh, which is dominated by Pine Hill on the south and Bear Mountain on the northwest. A. T. Shorey wrote that this was the site of a shoe peg factory worked many years ago by one Tub Mill, hence the name Tubmill Marsh. More likely the name derived from a James Tubs who settled in 1804 near the outlet of Paradox Lake.

From the fork to Tubmill Lean-to the blue trail continues downhill to cross a stream at 2.35 miles. Next, a small rise leads to a level at 2.55 miles. Honey Pond is visible on the left at 2.7 miles. Since the first edition of this guide, it has doubled in size, with many drowned trees, all due to beaver activity.

The trail is now circling to the east of Pine Hill, and at 2.8 miles a sign points to that hill, indicating a good spot to begin a bushwhack, section 81. The trail continues climbing, gently, on the flanks of Pine Hill, following the outlet of Lilypad Pond. You reach a level stretch at 3.1 miles, and 40 yards across it reach the intersection with the red trail to Lilypad Pond, 0.1 mile to the left. A lean-to sits on a rise overlooking that pond, which has also been enlarged in recent years, with many drowned trees rimming its shoreline.

The blue trail continues west to circle Horseshoe and Crab ponds on the way to Crane Pond, section 71.

76 Lilypad Pond to Rock Pond

Hiking, camping
1.2 miles, 1.2 hours, 150-foot elevation change

From the intersection of the blue trail just west of Lilypad Pond, section 75, a red trail heads generally east to Rock Pond. Beyond the Lilypad Pond Lean-to, the red trail quickly swings northeast to round Peaked Hill. In 0.1 mile it begins a gradual descent through a beech dieback area that has opened the forest to maple and viburnum starts. Only a narrow footpath is visible.

At 0.4 mile the trail reaches the level of a swamp surrounding Rock Pond Brook. There is a lovely view of Potter Mountain across the swamp, which can be a birdwatcher's paradise. Beaver work here forces the trail to higher ground and can make the walking a bit wet. The swamp has a bare stump forest in fields of waving grass with giant pine around the edge dotting the skyline.

The trail begins the climb away from the swamp at 0.55 mile and follows Rock Pond Brook all the way to the pond. Just after you begin the ascent, leave the trail to the left to explore the falls. A narrow footpath leads below a ledge to the top of the falls. A series of short cascades and pools combines to make about a fifty-foot vertical plunge.

The trail follows the brook for the next 0.3 mile, with the steep ledges of Peaked Hill coming almost down to the trail. At 0.95 mile a slippery log bridge takes the trail across a brook that flows from a draw between Peaked Hill and Big Clear Pond Mountain. This stream has a small but pretty waterfall that fades to insignificance in low water. A beautiful fern meadow borders the trail on the north. The bridge marks the beginning of the Peaked Hill bushwhack, section 80.

A gentle ascent follows, then the trail becomes level in the last 0.25 mile approach to Rock Pond. At 1.2 miles, the red trail intersects a red trail to the north side of Rock Pond, and another red trail continues around the south side, section 86.

Near Top of Bear Mountain — Pharaoh Mountain in Background

77 Bear Mountain
Bushwhack

Bear Mountain is a fault block with a west-facing cliff whose views offer an inviting bushwhack. The northwestern quadrant of Bear Mountain is privately owned, but it is possible to bushwhack to the top of the cliffs overlooking both Tubmill Marsh and Crane Pond and stay on state land all the way. From the height-of-land of the Tubmill Marsh Trail, 1.8 miles from NY 74, see section 74, a forty-five minute walk at most, take a compass course of 277° magnetic. This course, about halfway between magnetic and due west, will take you up the long eastern slope of Bear Mountain. It will keep you below the summit, on state land, and let you wind across the long ridge, picking out the greatest number of open rock patches on the way. The boundary line runs generally east-west, south of and below the summit, crossing at 1600 feet elevation.

Besides the overlooks of Tubmill Marsh on the way west, you will find a perch on the western edge, on top of the steep western cliffs, overlooking the eastern end of Crane Pond. Pharaoh Mountain fills the southern skyline.

It is 1 mile from the trail to the western cliffs on Bear Mountain, but you will wind about a bit between open patches on the way. Allow an hour for the 300 foot climb from the trail to the western perch.

An alternate, a real scramble, can be made from the far northeastern bay of Crane Pond. The spot is easiest if approached by water. A stiff, 500-foot climb in 0.4 mile will take you to the western perch. Your route should be to the east of the cliff line on the sharp nose and the direction for the bushwhack is toward magnetic north.

78 Potter Mountain
Bushwhack

This bushwhack is sufficiently short that it can easily be combined with a bushwhack on Ragged Mountain, section 79. Walk to the height-of-land on the Tubmill Marsh Trail and descend from it toward the marks, no more than 50 yards. There is a sign labeled "Potter Mtn." at the spot, 1.95 miles from NY 74, but signs have a way of disappearing. The walk to this point is just under an hour.

A course of almost due east takes you quickly to the western slopes of the mountain. You cross an old woods road on the way; it led around to the south of the mountain. Climb to the east, up the long shoulder of Potter. You will probably run into cairns marking an informal footpath on the way up and along the summit ridge. You reach open patches above the 1500-foot level, then continue winding on open rock to about 1800 feet. You accomplish the 500-foot climb in 0.5-mile walk from the trail, and you will be surprised how quickly you reach the summit ridge, even if you do not intersect the path with cairns.

Continue walking along the summit ridge contouring in a gentle arc that curves to the northeast. The ridge slopes gently down from the 1800-foot level, offering changing views that continue for another 0.4 mile. Cairns lead along the summit ridge. You will see Pine and Peaked hills, with Big Clear Pond Mountain between them in a row across the south. Most of Gooseneck Pond is visible. It should take you no more than an hour to reach the farthest vantage on the northeast end of the summit.

Historical notes tell of an iron mine opened on Potter Mountain by Walter Chilson in the early 1800s, but this mine was never worked.

79 Ragged Mountain
Bushwhack

Ragged is another superb little mountain. Who can believe views that begin after only a ten-minute climb? As you first approach the height-of-land 1.8 miles from NY 74 on the Tubmill Marsh Trail, take a course toward 35° magnetic. This takes you through open hemlock forest on level ground. You contour around several small hillocks and draws, crossing an old log road (it takes an expert to spot this one), and a sphagnum seep. In 0.2 mile you are at the foot of Ragged Mountain below ledges that make a fairly steep climb up the long shoulder. Head toward magnetic north, keeping back, east, from the steepest ledges. They are impossible to climb, and even this route is a bit of a scramble, but in just five minutes you have a view of Pharaoh Mountain. Small pine and birch fill niches on the nubble hillside. As you clamber over ledges you will probably see the charred stumps of a long ago fire.

You can see the corner of Pyramid Lake from the first level you reach. That level is the top of a long, exposed ridge. Behind it you begin a second scramble that brings you to the ridge line below the summit. There are spectacular views from this series of ledges that is only 200 feet above

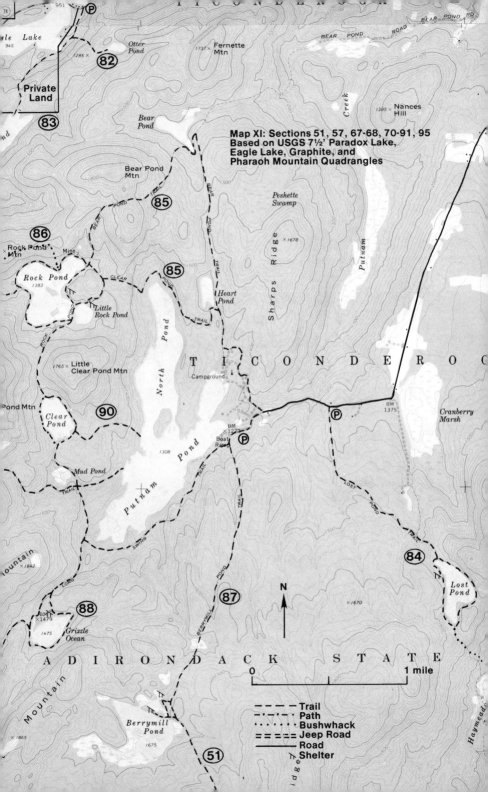

Map XI: Sections 51, 57, 67-68, 70-91, 95
Based on USGS 7½' Paradox Lake,
Eagle Lake, Graphite, and
Pharaoh Mountain Quadrangles

N

0   1 mile

- - - - Trail
· · · · · Path
· · · · · · Bushwhack
= = = = Jeep Road
——— Road
Shelter

the trail. Blue Hill presents a sharp face beyond Pyramid Lake. Over one corner of Pyramid Lake you can see Hoffman Mountain with Vander-whacker to the left of Hoffman. Pharaoh is in the south-southwest, and to the north or right of Pharaoh lie Meadow and Carey Hills. Potter is close on the southeast with a shoulder of Treadway visible beyond Potter's western flank. Red and white pine take twisted shapes near the ridge line where bearberry fills the niches between open rock slabs. Continue walk-ing along the ridge line, generally to the northwest, enjoying the chang-ing views.

At the end of the ridge you can begin to descend from the mountain by heading toward magnetic north. It is wise to go a bit east to avoid the steepest slopes, but do not go so far east you miss another vantage point. This last one, a small opening on top of a ledge, is between 100 and 150 feet below the summit ridge. From it you can see Moxham Ridge and Hoff-man Mountain, and to the right of Hoffman, the eastern High Peaks rang-ing around to Giant and Rocky Peak Ridge. It is easy to spot Nippletop and the Dixes, with Boreas in the foreground leading back around to Hoff-man. From this point you have the best view of Pyramid Lake.

Walk a little east and head downhill when it seems reasonable, heading generally north and picking the easiest way. A route to the north will in-tersect one leg of the Tubmill Marsh Trail. The farther east you go, the less steep the mountain becomes. However, it is not difficult to traverse across the open hillside beneath tall red pine and cedar, though you will find the needle-covered hillside slippery.

Just about the steepest reasonable descent will bring you out near the intersection of the old and new trails, a descent of 400 feet in a little more than 0.2 mile. The entire walk across the summit and back to the trail should take only an hour, making it reasonable that this trip can be walked as an extension of the trip up Potter Mountain.

Since so many of these bushwhacks are desirable for snowshoers, it should be noted the climb at the top of this one, especially in icy conditions, makes this an almost impossible winter trip.

80 Peaked Hill
Bushwhack

The easiest bushwhack to the summit of Peaked Hill starts from the Lilypad Pond-Rock Pond Trail, section 76. Find the bridge over the small stream

Ragged Mountain

that flows from the draw between Peaked Hill and Big Clear Pond Mountain. The bridge is 0.95 mile east of Lilypad Pond Lean-to and 0.25 mile west of the intersection of the red trails on the west shore of Rock Pond.

Follow the west side of this small stream; if you use the east side for a guide you may become confused by another, even smaller, intermittent stream coming from Big Clear Pond Mountain. The valley leads to a saddle between the mountains in about 0.75 mile. You will notice that the Peaked Hill slopes on your right begin to form a ridge that is open on the top. Climb up on the ridge and follow it back north to the summit of Peaked Hill.

This slightly circuitous route avoids the steepest climbing on Peaked Hill and is suitable for snowshoeing in winter. In summer, a frontal attack is possible, taking a course of 220° magnetic from the bridge. It requires a bit of scrambling and is fairly steep, rising 650 feet in 0.45 mile.

The view is superb: Rock Pond to the east and Rock Pond Mountain north, following around west to Potter and Bear mountains. On a clear day the High Peaks can be seen in the distant north-northwest.

Open rock slabs cover the entire summit. All the surrounding hills and valleys must have looked like this after the glaciers melted. A sharp ledge at the summit surmounts the "peak," and sharp cliffs fall away to the northwest. Open rock slides range on the northern slopes almost all the way down to the Lilypad Pond-Rock Pond Trail.

81 Pine Hill
Bushwhack

Pine Hill may be the gem of the small trailless peaks; its view is great and its climb is another easy bushwhack. Walk south on the Tubmill Marsh-Lilypad Pond Trail for 2.8 miles from NY 74. The walk should take an hour and a quarter and is described in section 75. The spot may be marked, but if it is not, it is easy to locate since it is just 0.1 mile south of Honey Pond and 0.3 mile north of the trail intersection that is northwest of Lilypad Pond.

Take a course toward 245° magnetic. The climb to the west-southwest takes you up 600 feet in under 0.5 mile. It is a moderately steep climb, but you reach an open summit with views in all directions. In fact, for such a small mountain, there is a surprising amount of space to explore on the open summit. In the north, you can pick out Bald Pate, Owl Pate,

Pyramid Lake from Bear Mountain

Pharaoh Mountain from Bear Mountain

and Hail, the highest peak east of the Northway. The latter mountain lies directly behind Port Henry. All of the nearby peaks are visible: Bear, Potter, Ragged in the north, Treadway and Big Clear Pond mountains, and Peaked Hill ranging from southeast to east. The latter peaks cut off distant views to the southeast, but in every other direction the views seem limitless.

On a clear day you feel as if you can reach out and touch Pharaoh Mountain, which lies to the southwest, with Crane Mountain in the distance to the right of it. Of the little ponds, Alder, Crane, Crab, Horseshoe, Rock, and Gooseneck are visible. Best of all, the cut north of Hoffman frames the High Peaks, with Marcy, Haystack, the Dixes, Giant, and Rocky Peak Ridge all identifiable.

It is amazing how much you can see from this 1900-foot hill. What a marvelous perspective it gives of the surrounding hills and ponds! The view is every bit as good as that from the higher summits of Pharaoh and Treadway, and the bushwhack is so easy that you do not even miss having a trail.

Allow an hour and a half for the round trip from the trail near Honey Pond. The entire round trip walk from NY 74 should take about five hours.

Putnam Pond

INDUSTRY IS THE key to the eastern section of the Pharaoh Lake Wilderness around Putnam Pond. Early industry dug into the mountains and consumed the forests, and the early industrialists left their names on the region's communities, mountains, and ponds. After the Revolutionary War, settlers from Vermont crossed Lake Champlain to the eastern Adirondack foothills. From Ticonderoga they moved inland to farm, log, and explore for minerals and ores.

The first families, the Blackmans and the Chilsons, settled near modern NY 74 where a small settlement is now called Chilson. Between 1800 and 1850, others arrived, creating a number of industries. On the outlet of Putnam Pond, officially Putnam Creek but locally known as Putt's Creek, several sawmills were built. At the outlet of the pond, H. and T. Treadway milled the lumber from their vast holdings, lands that stretched far south of Putnam Pond to Pharaoh Lake. The area's second tallest peak, Treadway, is named for this family. The first lumber taken from the shores of Pharaoh Lake was hauled north to Putnam Pond and out to market through Chilson and Ticonderoga. Most logs were floated in rafts, and lumber was transported by barge south along Lake Champlain. With the opening of the canal from Lake Champlain to the Hudson in 1823, logs and lumber were easily carried south to New York City. The lumber mill by the dam at the outlet of Putnam Pond was in operation through the end of the nineteenth century, finally closing in 1905.

There were mills at Berrymill Pond, Cranberry Marsh, and Bear Pond. Power from Gooseneck Pond ran a mill in the western bay of Eagle Lake.

After 1826, when iron was discovered in the hills to the north of modern NY 74, natives turned to the production of charcoal, which was produced by burning logs either in huge earthen pits or in large brick kilns. There were kilns at Cranberry Marsh and Lost Pond.

French woodcutters arrived in 1840 and built a mill and a kiln at French settlement, south of Chilson, on Putnam Creek. Peshette Swamp and Nances Hill record their influence.

Somewhere near Chilson was a depression in a ledge where water collected. The water reputedly cured warts and attracted people from long distances.

Graphite had been mined near Ticonderoga and Hague in the later 1800s, but it was not until 1901 that it became profitable to try to recover graphite from the strike on the northern shores of Rock Pond. You can see the stumps of fallen forest giants. But, unless you search about for clues to the early settlers, your dominant impression will be of the recovery of the wilderness.

With two exceptions all the trails in this chapter are reached from Putnam Pond or the road to it from Chilson. The two exceptions have trailheads on the western lobe of Eagle Lake. Chilson is 13.3 miles east of Northway Exit 28 on NY 74, 4.9 miles west of NY 22 at Ticonderoga. At Chilson a sign directs you south to the Putnam Pond State Campsite. The road bends east and at 3.2 miles passes the Lost Pond Trailhead. The campsite entrance is 0.4 mile beyond. Follow the signs through the campground to a parking area for day hikers 0.45 mile from the entrance.

Putnam Pond has an excellent state campsite with very good facilities. It is usually not crowded and is perhaps the best base from which to make day trips into the Pharaoh Lake Wilderness.

82 Otter Pond

Hiking, fishing
0.45 mile, ½ hour, 350-foot elevation change

The trail to Otter Pond traditionally has begun on a private road on the eastern side of the west lobe of Eagle Lake. There is no parking at the trailhead and problems have arisen. This trail and the one to Gooseneck Pond, section 83, begin from the access road to Ticonderoga's water supply. This road is just past the first house east of Eagle Lake Causeway on the south side of NY 74. The route is not currently posted.

One possible approach is to park, with permission, on NY 74 near the causeway and walk south on the macadam road to a barrier at 0.1 mile. A short pitch beyond the barrier leads to a fork where a private road heads right, 0.2 mile south of the barrier. The way left is clearly marked as part of the Pharaoh Lake Wilderness Area. Near the top of the short rise, the trail splits. Take the left fork, and at 0.25 mile, after a 30 yard descent, you will have to look closely to find the fork left to Otter Pond.

The DEC plans to designate an alternate beginning for the trail in the future. The trailhead will be at the southeastern corner of the west lobe of Eagle Lake where state land touches the lake. To reach this point, you will have to paddle east across Eagle Lake from the state boat launch facilities adjacent to NY 74. This launching site is near the outlet of Eagle Lake and has parking for a few cars.

From the waterside trailhead, walk northeast along the water company road for 0.1 mile to the Otter Pond Trail. This segment of roadway is entirely on state land. A fork right at 0.1 mile puts you on the blue-marked trail. You cross an intermittent stream and head right up the streambed at a moderate grade, part of which is a 200-foot climb in less than 0.2 mile.

At 0.2 mile, the trail leaves the streambed and continues on the north side for 100 yards before it rejoins the streambed. You pass a large boulder and the trail moderates, becoming level at 0.35 mile. The trail swings south around a wet area and reaches the pond at its outlet at 0.45 mile.

A steep hillside encircles the eastern end of the pond. If you walk around to the north about 100 yards, you will find a rock outcrop with a fine view of the pond. This is a good picnic spot. An unmarked path continues around the pond to the steep cliffs on the eastern end. You may find good fishing, since the pond is stocked with trout.

83 Gooseneck Pond

Hiking, fishing
0.6 mile, ½ hour, 290-foot elevation change

Access to the wilderness land that surrounds all but a small piece of the northern shoreline of Gooseneck Pond is complicated. That northern shoreline has a dam and outlet flume for a water line that serves the Town of Ticonderoga. The town owns all the land north along the old access road from Eagle Lake to Gooseneck Pond. The road is barred to vehicles and is not posted, but camping, fishing, and fires are prohibited on water company property. The town is currently trying to extend these prohibitions to Gooseneck Pond and its shoreline.

The DEC recommends approaching the pond by first launching a canoe at the boat ramp site on NY 74 near the outlet of Eagle Lake. A point on the south shore, 0.25 mile east of the boat launch is on state land. From it you can bushwhack south over the shoulder of Potter Mountain to the pond, generally following the property line.

Alternatively, the access road, which is not posted, can be reached by water. It will have the same beginning as the access to Otter Pond, section 82. At the southeast corner of Eagle Lake, where the roadway is on state land, head south, quickly reaching water company land. Vehicles have destroyed the roadway, but the road had its revenge! A hopelessly stuck hulk lies rusting and mired in deep mud not far from the lake.

As the road pulls away from the lake, it passes the surging standpipe of the waterworks, then cuts steeply uphill through a draw with ledges on both sides. A switchback on the left leads to a second draw that marks the end of the rise. A fork in the road follows. The way left leads to the flume at the outlet where a deep channel has been blasted away to create the water intake. The way right almost parallels the way left, but reaches the shoreline on state land.

Gooseneck Pond is a faulted rock basin, and the ledges on the southeastern shore along the fault line are its most handsome feature. Pine trees alternate with open patches on the steep southeast shore. There is an informal path along the northwest shore. Here, you walk along a narrow ridge that drops off on both sides, passing enormous charred pine stumps on the way. The open pine stand that now covers the burn area makes easy walking along the shore to a point from which you can see the neck of the 1.25-mile-long, thin, pond. The pine and needle covered dry slopes also make this a high fire danger area.

If, in the future, the roadway access is posted, or if fishing, boating and camping are prohibited on the pond, you will find it is certainly a handsome enough destination to warrant a bushwhack to this northwestern shore following the property line from Eagle Lake.

84 Lost Pond

Hiking, fishing, camping, cross-country skiing
1.35 miles to the pond, 1.25 mile loop around the pond, 2½ hour circuit, 200-foot elevation change

Lost Pond is a very handsome body of water. It has a lean-to and several campsites and a reputation as a good trout pond, with, as the ranger says, the garbage to testify to its popularity. It once had a charcoal kiln to produce charcoal for the Penfield Iron Works at Ironville, and there were nearly a dozen homesteads here until 1895.

The trailhead, where there is limited parking, is 3.2 miles south of Chilson on the Putnam Pond Campground road. The yellow marked trail heads south with a gradual but gently uphill grade. At 0.55 mile, the trail drops sharply to cross a wet area, then climbs again to cross an intermittent stream at 0.7 mile. The route continues gradually uphill to a plank bridge at 1 mile. Beyond it corduroy paves the trail. At 1.1 miles, a trail juncture left leads to a piped spring and private land. Take the way right that heads uphill, then levels, and at 1.35 miles reaches the pond and a fork in the trail.

Lost Pond Lean-to

The marked trail circles the pond in a 1.25 mile loop. For a counter-clockwise walk around the pond, turn right. You pass the lean-to in 0.1 mile, then walk beneath a rock cliff. Halfway round the pond you reach the first campsite with a fireplace. The small peninsula that follows also has a fireplace and is the best picnic spot on the pond. A third picnic spot is off the trail to the right at 0.8 mile.

The trail crosses a low spot, then heads back up the northeastern shore where the slopes of Abes Hill drop precipitously to water level, forcing the trail uphill. The walking is difficult, but you climb a steep pitch to several large boulders from which there are beautiful views of the pond. There are reported to be extensive caves on this mountainside.

You wind along the rocky shoreline, then drop to water level and a fire ring 0.1 mile from the trail intersection. An outhouse is next, and almost back at the intersection you pass a fifth fireplace, which is near a small, sandy beach.

Lost Pond is the best access for bushwhackers seeking to explore the Bald Ledge Primitive Area to the east. The top of Blanchard Mountain to the southeast is state land and cliffs with views range below the summit. Proposed acquisitions may make it possible to visit others among the open peaks in this Primitive Area. Some have views west into the Pharaoh Lake region, others overlook Lake Champlain.

85 Putnam Pond Loop to Heart, Bear, and Rock Ponds

Hiking, camping, fishing, swimming, cross-country skiing
5.4 mile loop, 3 hours, 430-foot elevation change

This circular walk, in which only the segment north to Heart Pond is repeated, takes you past several mine pits and a campsite where rough cabins once housed graphite miners and millworkers. The Rock Pond Mine was only one of several pits opened on the slopes of Bear Pond Mountain. However, the Bly Pits on the north side of the mountain were never developed. If you extend this walk by exploring Rock Pond Mine, section 86, add an hour to the estimated time.

The circuit is also a fine nature walk with a variety of ponds, waterfronts, and forest cover that induces a wide range of trailside plants.

From the day hiker's parking area at the Putnam Pond Campground, walk generally north through the campground to Campsite 38. It will take you 15 minutes to cross the campsite area. Trail measures start at the beginning of the blue-marked trail, which is an extension of a paved road, but quickly (100 feet) turns right to follow a little brook. (Note that some DEC maps designate this as a yellow trail.) At first there are as many rocks in the trail as in the brook. Small hemlock and birch, second and third-growth stands line the way. Red and painted trillium bloom along the trail in late May when spring flooding will make this crossing of the outlet of Heart Pond difficult. The blue trail turns right at 0.35 mile and heads north over a split log bridge. The way left, yellow, leads past North Pond and will be the return route for this circuit. To walk the loop in a counter-clockwise direction, head north toward Bear Pond on the blue trail.

You glimpse only a small portion of Heart Pond through the trees, then take a relatively level and straight course north for 1.2 miles. The trail has a nice narrow foot tread, and along the way you will find large white birch, mayflowers, white violets, spring beauties, Dutchman's-breeches, crinkle root, and a few wet places which will disappear with the spring flowers. One pine-filled burn area is carpeted with trailing arbutus and clumps of partridge berry, golden thread, and wintergreen. A stretch of particularly good woods has several varieties of *lycopodia* standing shinily green against the soft grey mats of lichens. Only fire could have produced this thin soil and the rock ledges that make this woods special. The patches of blueberries are right at home.

Peaked Hill from Rock Pond

At 1.5 miles the trail curves left and descends fairly steeply. Bear Pond is visible through the trees. You cross the old road from Chilson, which was the main access to the graphite mines. The way right, to Chilson, now leads to private lands. Your trail turns left and follows the roadway.

You have to leave the trail to appreciate the pond. A knoll beside the trail has a nice campsite. There are rock ledges on the pond's western end, but the east is filled with marshes and a beaver house.

At 1.7 miles the trail crosses the swampy eastern end of the pond where a camp was located when graphite was mined. The trail hugs the hillside, because the beaver have flooded the old road. If you look carefully on the left of the trail, near the marsh, you may spot a pit or an old cellar hole. Angle right at the end of the marsh, crossing an intermittent stream, and begin to climb the slopes of Bear Pond Mountain. You pass a test pit on the way up. Oak fern and foam flower and mitrewort line the trail. An intermittent stream glistens with the iron pyrites that typify the local graphite ore.

You meet an unmarked intersection and continue left. The way right is the abandoned road that led past the Eutoka Pit and up the north slopes of Bear Pond Mountain to the Joan Pit. All are continuations of the same graphite-bearing ore.

If you are looking closely, you will spot another pit on the right side of the trail just beyond the intersection. The trail rises to a saddle at 2.6 miles. The draw at the top of the saddle is sheltered by a pine-covered knoll on the southeast. The trail picks up an intermittent stream on the north side of the saddle and follows it for a time. You begin a descent to Rock Pond, and at 3 miles, the trail passes the foundations of the mine supply house on the right and an indistinct road on the left. See section 86 for a guide to exploring the graphite mine that is to the west of the trail.

The trail drops steeply to Rock Pond and an intersection with the red trail at 3.1 miles. The trail west around Rock Pond is also described in section 86. Turn left and follow the red trail for only 60 yards south through the swampy area to the intersection with the yellow trail east. You can take that left fork trail to complete the circuit, intersecting the Clear Pond-North Pond Trail in 0.15 mile.

Alternatively, you can circle south around a knoll on the red trail that follows the shore of Rock Pond to the lean-to in 0.2 mile. At a second intersection at 0.3 mile you would head east on the Clear Pond-North Pond Trail, past Little Rock Pond and its lean-to. Little Rock Pond is small enough that its waters are usually quiet, providing a reflecting pool for the birch and pine that surround the pond. From Little Rock Pond Lean-to it is 0.2 mile northeast around the knoll to join the left fork mentioned above. The extra 0.55-mile circuit has enough interest to make it worth-while.

East of the intersection, the yellow trail takes you back to the blue trail near Heart Pond in 1.2 miles. The total walk, with the detour to Little Rock Pond, will be 5.4 miles.

Picking up the trail, at the yellow intersection at 3.8 miles, the Clear Pond-North Pond Trail makes a gentle ascent for 0.25 mile to a divide, part of the line that separates the Champlain and Hudson watersheds. Just over 0.1 mile farther, at 4.15 miles, you reach the closest approach to North Pond, but you have to leave the trail for a 0.1-mile walk to the shoreline following a trail also marked with yellow. The main yellow trail circles the northern shore of North Pond, crossing an inlet at 4.4 miles and head-ing south for a short rise to a height-of-land at 4.65 miles. After circling the ridge, the trail swings back north to drop south to Heart Pond. The intersection at just over 5 miles is 0.1 mile to the east. The loop ends by retracing the blue trail south 0.35 mile to Putnam Pond Campground.

86 Rock Pond and Rock Pond Mountain and Mine

Hiking, camping, exploring old mine sites
1.9-mile circuit, 3 hours, relatively level except the optional bushwhack to the mountain

It does not take three hours to circle Rock Pond, but you will want to allow that long so you can visit the abandoned graphite mine on the north shore. Section 85 details approaches to Rock Pond, the shortest of which is 1.75 miles from Putnam Pond Campground.

In 1901 a mine was opened at the deposit on the slopes of Bear Pond Mountain behind the northeastern bay of Rock Pond. In the next five years a block of ore, faulted on all sides, was removed to a depth of 40 feet. Ore, 3,000 pounds a day, was hauled from the mine up an incline and down to a mill built above the shore of the pond. Here a ten stamp mill crushed the ore, mixed it with water, and fed it to buddles in which the ore was separated and shoveled out through the top. Tailings were shoveled from the bottom and spread in piles near the mill area. Steam heaters dried the ore, which was then hauled to Ticonderoga for further milling.

To explore the mill, walk west from the intersection of the blue Bear Pond Trail following the red trail on Rock Pond's northeastern corner. A huge metal cylinder, the steam boiler, sits above the trail 100 yards from the intersection. Northwest of the boiler you can trace the beginning of the stone foundations of the three-story, 50 by 135-foot mill building. Thick cedar planks span the mortared rock walls.

If you continue west along the trail for 80 yards, you reach the end of the drainage tunnel from the mine, a cave-like opening six feet square. Turn up the hillside to follow the stream, which falls prettily beside the tunnel. The streambed is stained red with iron oxides, for the ore was a "feldspar schist carrying the graphite and heavily impregnated with pyrite." Between the stream and the upper level of the ruins, you can find piles of tailings and the circular ruins of a small brick building. Follow the stream uphill for 100 yards to the open mine pit.

The 150-foot diameter circular hole with vertical sides (the vein of ore stood in a nearly vertical strike) is filled with turquoise water tinted by copperas and giving off a strong odor. The walls of the pit are stained red and yellow and rust browns from the oxides, hydroxides, and sulfates of iron found in the ore. The picture seems more suited to a pool on a Caribbean Island than to an Adirondack landscape.

You can trace the mill road from the back of the three-story building to the west toward the pit, then uphill and back east in a switchback that intersects the modern Bear Pond Trail, 0.1 mile from the red-blue intersection that begins this loop. East of the blue trail, opposite the road, you will find the foundations of a supply house built into the hillside.

After you have explored the mine, return to the mine tunnel at water level and continue walking west on the red marked trail. The entire north shore is rocky and steep, and the trail is narrow and occasionally difficult to follow as it swings up and down over ledges that drop to shoreline.

There is a lovely picnic site, 0.3 mile from the intersection on a smooth rock slab that slopes gently to water level. Swimming is good here, and you can even swim to the rock edged tiny islands that lie directly south of the promontory. The mountain you can see on the west-southwest is Peaked Hill.

Rock Pond Mountain lies behind you on the northwest, and it also has open rock ledges with views. Most of the openings face south, looking across to Peaked, Big Clear Pond, and Little Clear Pond mountains. If you have an hour to spare, take a detour bushwhack up Rock Pond Mountain. The gentlest approach from the pond is northwest up the ridge that extends to the campsite point. A very short, 300-yard scramble takes you up 200 feet in elevation to open rock. Turn west, then southwest, following the

Graphite Mine Boiler at Rock Pond

rock outcrops for better vantages. You reach a point from which it seems you can almost touch the rock slides on the northeast side of Peaked Hill. Retrace your route to the shore of Rock Pond and pick up the pond circuit again.

Continuing west, the trail drops to shoreline at 0.45 mile and is hard to follow. For the next 0.3 mile there are many lovely rock outcrops along the shore. At 0.75 mile you pass another good campsite, and 50 yards beyond, you reach the junction with the Lilypad Pond red trail.

To finish the circuit of the pond, turn left, east, also on a red trail for a 0.65 mile walk along the south shore. In 0.1 mile you reach another fine rock slab on a promontory thrust east into the pond. Ledges that follow are separated by thick carpets of needles and covered with bunchberry. You have lovely views of the ledges above on the north shore. As you turn south, ledges of Big Clear Pond Mountain drop almost to water level.

Beyond Rock Pond's southern lobe, marshes fill the inlet area. At 0.65 mile you reach the intersection with the yellow trails. The way right leads to Clear Pond, section 90. Go left, north for 120 yards to the outlet of Little Rock Pond; 75 yards beyond, a yellow trail forks right to Heart and Putnam ponds. The next 0.15 mile on the red trail north, the left fork, is currently very wet. You pass a campsite and the Rock Pond Lean-to. You walk at the end of the pond in a deep hemlock woods for 0.2 mile to another intersection, this one with the yellow trail east to Heart Pond. Continue straight ahead on the red trail, through a marsh and over a log bridge, for 50 yards to the intersection with the blue trail to Bear Pond where the circuit began.

87 Berrymill Pond from the North

Hiking, camping, fishing, excellent novice to intermediate cross-country ski trail
2 miles, 1¼ hours, 365-foot elevation change

Berrymill is a warmwater fish pond with good catches of bullhead, perch, and pike. Until the early 1970s, the roadway that the trail follows to the pond was used by sportsmen driving four-wheel-drive vehicles. This is no longer permitted. Two lean-tos make it a good camping and fishing destination.

The blue trail marked along the roadway starts from the south end of the hikers' parking area at the Putnam Pond Campground.

A gradual ascent leads in 0.65 mile to a plank bridge over a stream. The trail continues west of south to a wet area at 1.15 miles. Beyond it a slight uphill leads to swamps surrounding the pond's outlet stream. You pass the end of the swamp at 1.6 miles; just beyond, and 150 feet to the right of the trail, there is a waterfall on the stream. The trail crosses a small pool 0.1 mile beyond and begins to climb again, reaching the top of this grade at 1.85 miles. A path 0.1 mile beyond leads 400 feet across a small ravine to the northern lean-to. Just west of this lean-to a wheel at the outlet powered a sawmill which was owned in 1835 by Osier and Auger. At 2 miles the trail forks; the way right is the official trail to the same lean-to. A second intersection 120 yards beyond forks right to the second lean-to and left to a spring and the trail to West Hague Road, section 51.

88 Grizzle Ocean from Putnam Pond

Hiking, camping, fishing
1.9 miles, 1 hour, 164-foot elevation change

An easy walking, well-marked yellow and blue trail leads to and around Grizzle Ocean. If you add a circle of the pond and return to the Putnam Pond Campground, the whole trip should take no more than three hours. The trail begins from the southwest corner of the hiker's parking area and follows the shore of Putnam Pond for the first 0.15 mile. However, the trail is sufficiently far from the pond that there are only occasional glimpses of the water. Immediately south of the parking area, you cross a log bridge over an intermittent stream. At 0.15 mile a trail forks right to the shore of Putnam Pond. The trail crosses a second stream at 0.3 mile. Beyond the bridge the trail climbs around a hillside, which is very steep near the water. The climb takes you over the ridge and then back down at 0.85 mile to a bridge over the outlet stream of Berrymill Pond. In springtime the waterfalls upstream are lovely.

Your only real view of Putnam Pond is in the next 0.1 mile. The trail rounds a marsh at the southern end of the pond to cross another log bridge at 1 mile.

The trail now winds west with a moderate ascent on stone steps at 1.25 miles. At 1.35 miles the trail crosses the Grizzle Ocean's outlet stream. Forty feet beyond there is an intersection with a yellow trail, right, leading toward Clear Pond. You take the yellow trail headed south, uphill, beside the stream. A steady climb over a well-used trail takes you to a slippery log bridge that recrosses the outlet stream at 1.6 miles. At 1.75 miles the trail again forks. Here the yellow trail continues south toward Pharaoh Lake, and a blue trail heads left, east, around Grizzle Ocean.

The 1.1-mile circuit walk around the pond begins here. Your first view of the pond is at 1.9 miles when you reach the lean-to. Grizzle Ocean has some brook and rainbow trout, but not as many as in the past. The name of the pond is part of the area's lore. One Tom Grizzle discovered the pond and raved to his fellow loggers so much about his catches that his friends dubbed the place Grizzle's Ocean. There are beaver here, and most of the shoreline is wet with some dense spruce and hemlock thickets.

To circle the pond, head east on the blue trail that begins at shoreline below the lean-to. The trail makes a sharp turn south and passes one nice tent site before reaching a wet stream crossing at 0.3 mile. This inlet has no bridge. At 0.55 mile you may find the trail flooded, depending on beaver activity. The trail is close to shoreline all the way. You meet another wet place at the far end of the pond at 0.65 mile, and 0.1 mile later the yellow trail to Pharaoh Lake makes a sharp left turn.

If you continue straight on the trail (the markers are now yellow), you enter a small swamp that surrounds the outlet. A sinking log bridge at 75 yards takes you over the sphagnum mats that choke the outlet. Beyond, a dense hemlock thicket, as dark as night, covers part of the last 0.2 mile back to the intersection at the end of the circuit. Head right, northeast, on the yellow trail toward Putnam Pond to complete the 4.5 mile walk.

89 Pharaoh Lake from Grizzle Ocean

Hiking, camping
3.25 miles, 1½ hours, 330-foot elevation change

The sign at the intersection north of Grizzle Ocean states that it is 2.5 miles to Pharaoh Lake. The sign at Pharaoh Lake states that it is 2.4 miles to Grizzle Ocean Lean-to. It may be, as the crow flies, but unless you can walk on water you will cover 3.25 miles between the two points. If you reverse the trek and are carrying a pack, you will swear that even the corrected mileage is too short.

Walk south from the intersection for 0.2 mile through dense hemlock, turning to cross the outlet of Grizzle Ocean on a sinking log bridge. The logs take you over the sphagnum mats at the outlet. Turn south again for 75 yards to an intersection. A sharp right on the yellow trail heads toward Pharaoh Lake, and the trail is marked with yellow all the way. For the next 0.35 mile the trail passes through mixed hardwoods and hemlock in a narrow valley formed by two low ridges. At 0.6 mile the valley widens and the trail stays above and to the left of a small stream that originates in the valley. At 0.65 mile you cross the stream and follow a level ridge with the stream below and on the left. Tall and stately trees shelter the valley.

At 0.75 mile the trail begins to descend, shortly recrossing the stream. The narrow footpath shows hardly any signs of other hikers. The high ground on your right is the lower slopes of Grizzle Ocean Mountain.

At 1.05 mile another small stream appears on the right. You stay high above the stream as it drops rapidly off into a walled valley on the right. At 1.3 miles the trail again descends gently, and you are no longer aware of high ridges on your right. At 1.55 miles another small stream appears on your right, and just beyond, a larger one on your left. The trail goes sharply right, crossing the small stream that joins the larger one just beyond the crossing. The trail now alternately climbs and drops over a series of small ridges and hollows, descending to a log bridge over a wet seep at 1.8 miles.

You can now look through the hardwood forest to the valley below. Wide flows surround that valley, and the trail will make a sharp hairpin turn north to avoid them. At 1.85 miles a small waterway plunges over the ledge to your right. These ledges are extensions of Grizzle Ocean Mountain and mark the place the trail begins to turn north. A couple more

Roche Moutonne

Wintergreen Point—Pharaoh Lake

short ups and downs and the swamp is clearly visible on your left. Another small log bridge at 2.15 miles is followed by a bridge over the outlet of Devil's Washdish, that tiny pool high on the shoulder of Treadway.

Here the trail turns south, and you have lovely views of the ridges on Thunderbolt Mountain on your left. The completion of the hairpin turn is one of the most wonderful nature trails in the area. At one point the trail passes beneath ledges covered with dripping mosses. There is a sequence of ridges, the *roche moutonne*. Sometimes the trail is along those sheep backs, at other times it traces an undulating course up and over them. From the elevation of the little ridges, you are high and dry above the lovely beaver meadows and flows on your left. Bunchberry and Canada mayflower cover the ridges. There are ridges at 2.3 miles and 2.5 miles, and several in the next 0.25 mile, but the mileages are not important—just enjoy the views from them.

At 2.75 miles you cross a log bridge, then climb to the top of one of the sheep backs, about 15 feet high, where the view of the light greens of the meadows to the left contrasts with the deep greens of the hemlock that crown the ridge and fill the swampy hollows to the right of the trail. The area you are walking through was burned in the 1910 fire.

At 2.85 miles Wolf Pond is visible on the left. It is filled with water and lilies and pond weeds, and there are remarkably tall pines on the far shore. Shortly, you reach the end of the ridges that let you look over the alder-filled shores, and soon you are back in deep woods.

At 3.15 miles another small stream comes in from the right, and you can now hear the waterfalls on the outlet of Wolf Pond on your left. That stream has picked up the outlet of Devil's Washdish and drains into the long valley between Grizzle Ocean and Thunderbolt mountains. Now it pours these waters over a series of ledges that drop down to the shore of Pharaoh Lake.

You climb briefly away from the stream, then begin to see the lake through the trees, and at 3.2 miles start the final drop to shoreline and the trail intersection where all the trails are yellow.

The way right is the trail to Split Rock Bay and Crane Pond, the way left leads along the east shore of Pharaoh Lake. Directly ahead is the path to Wintergreen Point. All of these routes are described in section 58. No matter which way you turn you should walk south to the bridge over Wolf Pond Outlet for a view of the falls.

90 Clear Pond Trails

Hiking, camping, fishing, cross-country skiing
2 miles, 1 hour, 220-foot elevation change

The routes made possible by connectors with interior trails on the west side of Putnam Pond are detailed in section 92. Routes past Clear Pond are more than a means to reach other trails. They also lead to some lovely and unspoiled parts of the interior of the Pharaoh Lake Wilderness. The principal interior trail leads from the south end of Putnam Pond past Mud and Clear Ponds to Little Rock Pond.

From the south, at the bridge over Grizzle Ocean's outlet stream, section 88, take the blue trail headed north. A gentle ascent at 0.25 mile puts you high enough to overlook the marshes at the southern end of Putnam Pond. A second gentle crest leads down to a trail intersection at 0.4 mile. The way left is the red trail to Treadway, the way right leads to a landing on Putnam Pond. Both are described in the next section. For the next few yards, the trail is beside the outlet of Mud Pond where that stream flows through a handsome small gorge.

Mud Pond follows; it is a tiny marsh-shored pond. You follow its inlet north to an intersection at 0.8 mile, just south of Clear Pond. You can go left on a red trail along the western shore of the pond, but lack of use has left that route overgrown and difficult to follow. Immediately west of the trail intersection, the red trail crosses the outlet of Clear Pond where a big old log serves as a bridge. The trail turns sharply right to follow the shoreline, and in 100 yards reaches a high rock point that makes a good campsite. Continuing north, with few markers to guide the way, you pass a small waterfall at 0.3 mile and intersect the east shore trail again at 0.4 mile.

If you choose to go north on the blue trail, you reach the lean-to in less than 0.2 mile. It overlooks the clear, circular pond from a ledge, from which the swimming is good. The view across the pond to more ledges shows the lower slopes of Big Clear Pond Mountain.

There is a yellow trail behind the lean-to that leads back up to a landing on Putnam Pond. That short, 0.55 mile trail explains why so many people reach this lean-to.

If you wish to use this alternate to reach Clear Pond, you can find the trailhead on the shore of Putnam Pond by paddling west from Putnam Pond Campground. A large island marks the juncture of Putnam Pond and North Pond. West of the island on the western shore of Putnam Pond, a canoe access spot is marked with a signpost but no dock. A yellow-marked trail heads west from this waterfront trailhead, climbing through a mixed hardwood forest. At 0.2 mile the trail levels off and veers left, southwest, and at 0.3 mile crosses a log bridge over a small brook. You will first glimpse Clear Pond at 0.5 mile, then descend fifty yards to the lean-to.

The interior trail north of Clear Pond is now marked with yellow disks. It continues fairly close to shoreline beneath the steep slopes of Little Clear Pond Mountain, to intersect the red trail at 1.35 miles. The east side is 0.15 mile longer, but definitely easier to follow than the western one.

The trail begins the climb toward Rock Pond by entering a deep valley edged steeply on either side by the rounded rock ledges that typify the area. White birch and maple crown the height-of-land at 1.6 miles. In summer you should spot rattlesnake fern near the top of the hill. The trail makes a long traverse down the birch-covered hillside, and you can see water through the trees during most of the descent. At 2 miles the trail reaches the Rock Pond Trail junction. The way left is the red trail around the shore of Rock Pond, section 86. The way right leads past Little Rock Pond to intersect the trail toward North Pond and Putnam Pond Campground from the north, section 85.

Note that DEC maps indicate the south end of the interior trail is blue, the north end yellow, but both blue and yellow disks were found along all parts of the trail.

91 Treadway Mountain

Hiking, views
2.5 miles, 1½ hours, 830-foot elevation change

Treadway Mountain is a surprisingly good mountain. Its 2240-foot elevation may sound insignificant, and its 830-foot climb is certainly modest, but its views are neither. In fact, this may just be the most entrancing of any peak in the Pharaoh Lake Wilderness Area.

The trailhead is on the shore of Putnam Pond, 0.65 mile toward magnetic west from the campground boat launching area. If you do not have a canoe, you can walk south from the campground on the Grizzle Ocean Trail, section 88, then north from the intersection at the south of Putnam Pond on the Clear Pond Trail, section 90. That interior trail intersects the Treadway Trail 1.8 miles from the campground, adding 1.5 miles and at least forty-five minutes to the climb.

The same intersection can be reached from the north via the Heart Pond, North Pond, Little Rock Pond, Clear Pond route. This way is just over 3 miles longer and adds 1½ miles to the one-way trek. The round trip via the south is 8 miles and via the north is 11.1. A circuit of the ponds and a climb up Treadway is 9.5 miles long.

From the trailhead on the shore, the red-marked trail starts on the north side of Mud Pond Outlet, crossing it and several tributaries in the 0.3 mile to the intersection with the yellow and blue trail, section 90.

Beyond the intersection the red trail leads up a ledge south of the marshes on Mud Pond, then descends to a bridge over its inlet at 0.6 mile. The trail briefly follows the inlet, then heads northwest and uphill, a steady climb through a patch of hemlock and tall hardwoods to an intermittent stream on the right at 1.05 miles. This stream drains the saddle between Treadway and Big Clear Pond mountains and flows into Mud Pond. Its small flow, except during rains, attests to the way the burned and bare slopes of the two mountains retain little water.

You already should spot some quartz in the trail as you climb the small ledge. The narrow draw developing to the southeast at 1.5 miles is the headwaters of Devil's Washdish. You cross a log bridge at the head of the draw, and as you begin to climb again, cairns lead the way across open rock slabs. You can already see Big Clear Pond Mountain with its open rock. The trail winds between fire-scarred ledges with trailing arbutus and pink lady's slippers in the small niches between rock slabs. To the east you can see the back of the escarpment that outlines the Champlain Val-

Treadway Mountain

ley. It takes just over an hour to reach the first knob. Treadway's summit is surrounded with a cluster of small knobs. At the first, at 2 miles, the trail angles north, following a ridgeline to a second knob. As you cross its ridge, you can look across to the summit of Treadway and, southwest of it, to Pharaoh and Crane mountains.

The second knob, at 2.1 miles, is completely open, with rose quartz in many rock slabs. Some of the quartz has eroded, leaving strange, pock-marked slopes.

The trail winds between boulders and then turns abruptly west again, descending into a small but deep col, before reaching the summit. A fif-teen minute walk should suffice for the 0.4 mile walk from the second knob to the true summit. A broad panorama stretches to the south beyond Thunderbolt Ridge and Pharaoh Lake. To the east Mount Mansfield and Camel's Hump are identifiable in the long string of the Green Mountains of Vermont. To the northwest you will find that Hoffman's five mile length block quite a section of the horizon. Beyond its north end, you can spot Boreas and Pinnacle Ridge. Lining up on the horizon behind them are March, Haystack, Basin, Saddleback, Gothics, McComb, Dix, East Dix, Giant, and Rocky Peak Ridge, all beautifully silhouetted. On the western horizon you can see Blue Mountain, Snowy, and the top of Eleventh Moun-tain; continuing to the south, Moose, Baldhead, Crane and the mountains of Lake George, Black and the Tongue Mountain Range. This is one of the few places from which the whole stretch of Glidden Marsh is visible.

The open summit survives from the devastating fires of 1910 and 1911, which burned from Treadway south toward Pharaoh Lake.

92 The Long Walks and Bushwhacks

With the last day hike in the complex Pharaoh Lake Wilderness Area sys-tem described, you should be able to grasp the number of longer hikes avail-able. They include a winter snowshoe camping trek to the tops of eight or more peaks, a pond circuit that touches fifteen of the interior ponds, and a circuit of Pharaoh Lake.

The 7.5 minute USGS maps designate two good combination routes that have many camping possibilities: The Long Swing Trail commences at the western trailhead, section 68 on NY 74 and heads south to Crane Pond. It continues south to Pharaoh Lake, section 72, then north to Grizzle Ocean, section 89, and terminates at Putnam Pond, section 88. The Short Swing Trail utilizes the same trailhead but swings east from Glidden Marsh to pass Oxshoe, Crab, and Horseshoe ponds, section 71. It then turns north past Honey Pond and Tubmill Marsh, section 74, to intersect the eastern trailhead on NY 74.

Shorter trips include the circuit of Putnam Pond and the loop south of Crane past Glidden Marsh and Horseshoe and Oxshoe ponds.

Tremendous one-way treks can be made from West Hague Road through

Berrymill to Putnam Pond or northwest to NY 74 past a string of ponds. From Beaver Pond Road a one-way trek north over Pharaoh to Crane Pond and out to NY 74 is suggested.

Since all of the components of each trek have already been described and since there are many more good longer hikes than those indicated, I suggest that you become familiar with the trailheads and a few of the destinations and then design some of these treks for yourself.

As you walk through the Pharaoh Lake Wilderness, you cannot help but be impressed by the open peaks that invite bushwhack exploration. This guide only scratches the surface of the easiest bushwhacks. There are open patches on Big Clear Pond Mountain, and that peak is a short bushwhack across a high connecting ridge from Treadway. A drop from the summit toward the southern end of Clear Pond provides an easy way to make a loop walk. A loop over Peaked Hill and Big Clear Pond Mountain is also desirable.

Both Grizzle Ocean and Thunderbolt mountains have open patches and some views. The ultimate needle in the haystack is Devil's Washdish on the southeast slopes of Treadway.

You will find the more accessible places full of people, but this wilderness has an unbelievable range of little used trails and secret places to discover.

Iron Hills

WALKING NORTH OF NY 74 means traveling back in history to the time our ancestors were feverishly searching for iron ore and rushing to build forges and blast furnaces to manufacture iron. It means visiting hills where every tree was felled to make charcoal for the blast furnaces. So great was the forest destruction that a principal reason for the decline of iron manufacturing after 1875 was the shortage of charcoal. But, in the half century preceding, veins were opened on dozens of hills and numerous settlements emerged in the wilderness. Most of the settlements have returned to wilderness, and it is difficult to discover many of the mines, as they are privately owned and posted. But even the mountain walks that do not lead to mine sites remain rich with the history of the Adirondacks' industrial past.

93 Ironville and the Penfield Homestead
Walking tour

Ironville lies 3.5 miles north of NY 74 on County Route 2, which is 12.2 miles east of Northway Exit 28.

Iron was discovered in the hills five miles to the west of Ironville in 1826. Allen Penfield and Timothy Taft built a forge at Ironville in 1828. Putt's Creek was dammed to create the pond you pass on the way to Ironville, and its water was harnessed for power.

By 1873 there were five forges using charcoal to produce iron blooms, the rough product of the first smelting. A railroad was built in 1873 from Crown Point on the shores of Lake Champlain to Ironville and west to the settlement of Hammondville, which had grown up around the mines. Thirteen miles of track rose 1300 feet into the Adirondack foothills to retrieve the iron and the ore, which, after the building of the railroad, was taken to the blast furnaces at Crown Point.

Ironville was a company town. The home of its founder, Allen Penfield, is now a museum that tells the story of the mines, of the Penfield family life, and of the people who worked the mines. Photographs, many taken around 1875 by Seneca Ray Stoddard, have been enlarged and placed on maps that illustrate the three villages.

Not only is the operation of the forges described, but the museum tells of the birth of the Electric Age. Ironville was the site of the first industrial use of an electromagnet. Allen Penfield used an electromagnet built by Professor Joseph Henry of Albany to charge his magnetic iron ore separating machine.

A brochure available in the museum contains a map and details of the points on a self-guided walking tour. It directs you past the Harwood House, home of one of Penfield's partners; the church and parsonage; a boarding house; and an inn, houses and barns that survive from the first half of the nineteenth century. The tour's brochure will lead you along the bed of the railroad, past ruins of the Catalan Forge, the foundations of the charcoal shed, the scale pit, and the remains of the middle dam where water poured through a wooden flume to power an ore separator and crusher.

You can use picnic tables in the field at the foot of Penfield Pond after you visit the museum and make the 0.5 mile tour through the village. The museum is open daily except Monday from May 15 through October 15.

94 Hammondville

Hammondville has almost disappeared. The last family from this community of 300 left in 1910, and only stone walls, foundations, stone steps, cellars, and mine shafts remain. Because of the danger of the mine shafts, some of which are 400 feet deep, International Paper Company, which owns the site, has posted the land.

A short excursion, however, will give you a flavor of what is at Hammondville. Drive west from Ironville on Old Furnace Road. Just past the intersection with North Road, Old Furnace Road makes a sharp right turn. An abandoned road continues straight to Hammondville. One hundred yards north of the intersection on the right side of Old Furnace Road, you will find a slag heap from one of the earliest blast furnaces. The furnace stands 100 feet from the northwest corner of the intersection of the abandoned road and Old Furnace Road. The furnace consumed charcoal made from the surrounding forests and pictures from the 1870s show all the nearby hills completely bare.

Before the abandoned road to Hammondville becomes posted, you can see its unusual paving: the brilliant blue cobalt slag from the forges.

Blast Furnace between Ironville and Hammondville

95 Skiff Mountain and Arnold Pond

Shore trail, path, and bushwhack, hiking, exploring
0.3 mile to pond, 1 mile to mountain, 2 hours round trip, 850-foot
vertical rise

High quality iron ore was found on the slopes of Skiff Mountain above
Ore Bed Bay on Eagle Lake. Arnold P. Skiff explored a vein there in 1857,
but the difficulties of recovering the ore made mining it too expensive.
In spite of the cost, succeeding owners dug a tunnel to explore for other
veins at the base of the mountain. This walk does not approach the vein,
but it explores the discoverer's namesake mountain and pond.

NY 74 circles south around the steep slopes of Skiff Mountain, which
stretch between the head of Paradox Lake and the foot of Eagle Lake. There
is a marked official DEC trail to Arnold Pond, and an unofficial path marked
with flags and cairns to Skiff's summit ridge and across it through fields
of blueberries that crown the partially open summit. The northeast side
of the ridge is heavily wooded and posted private land. From the southern
slopes there are great views from north through west and south to the southeast.

To reach the trailhead, use one of the two parking areas on the south
side of NY 74. There are turnouts less than 0.1 mile east and 0.4 mile

west of the trailhead, which is 7.7 miles east of Northway Exit 28 or 1.7 miles west of the Eagle Lake Causeway.

The blue-marked trail starts straight up the face of the mountain, over one of the most rock strewn trails in the Adirondacks. The rocks are not exposed by hiker's feet; they are just typical of the glacial rubble that covers the whole south side of the mountain. The sharp ascent lasts for just over 0.2 mile, a climb of 250 feet. A level stretch is followed by a short rise to a ridge whose far side drops directly to the pond at 0.3 mile. You will find a beaver dam to the east of the outlet and a swampy, not exactly pretty, area. Huge beaver-chewed stumps line a footpath east. Walking west around the pond is not much better. A glacial cirque, encloses the northern shore; its arms thrust forward to encircle the pond on three sides. You can see the pond from boulders on the cirque, but beware. The most extensive poison ivy patch so far encountered in the Adirondacks lines the uphill sides of the boulder field.

There is a better way to view the pond. At the crest of the ridge south of the pond, about 100 feet from shoreline, look carefully. A small footpath with tin can lids and some blue paint daubs leads along the ridge to the west, curving around and following open patches up the western side of the cirque. The path, naturally placed on high ground, follows the nose of the mountain and steadily curves back east to reach Skiff's summit ridge from its western end. Cairns mark the upper half of the path; they are not close, but placed at about 50 foot intervals. If you should lose the path here, the way is open enough for an easy bushwhack climb.

Rusty woodsia fern, marginal shield fern, and sweetfern shrub edge the open rock patches. Blueberries are everywhere.

From the western end of the ridge you can see Pyramid Lake and its tiny, cone-shaped island. The steep flanks of Blue Hill and Bear Mountain make a deep shelter for that lake. Beyond lies Pharaoh Mountain. You can look over the long axis of Paradox Lake to see Peaked Hill north of it. Hoffman Mountain blocks the distant west. Owl Pate marks the northern limit of the view, but to the left of it range the High Peaks.

As you walk east across the ridge, being careful to stay south of the private land, you overlook Ragged and Potter Mountains, which seem to conceal Treadway. From the top of the cirque, you look directly down into Arnold Pond.

The hills north of NY 74 are a nesting place for the American kestral, that small, brilliantly colored falcon with swallow-shaped wings. Kestrals are usually spotted on Severance and Peaked hills and here on Skiff Mountain. In midsummer you may be as fortunate as I was and observe an adult pair teaching their three juveniles to dart and dive and hunt.

The informal path marked with cairns leads east between open rock

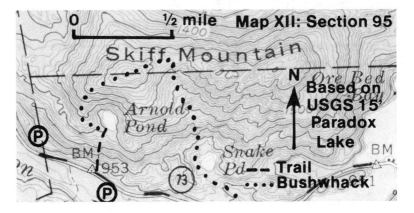

patches and blueberry clumps across the western summit. It gradually disappears, but you can easily continue walking east along the summit ridge until you are directly above Snake Pond, a distance of about 0.2 mile. Instead of retracing your steps, you can begin to make your way down the steep draw that leads to Snake Pond. This bushwhack makes a delightful variation of the Skiff Mountain climb and you may even spot the entrance to an old mine tunnel on the way.

A twenty-minute descent of just over 0.5 mile takes you down the 550-foot descent to Snake Pond, which is surrounded by a bog filled with pitcher plants. The pond's outlet on the southeast corner can serve as a guide for the 0.25 mile descent to NY 74. That stream emerges not far from the boat launching site on Eagle Lake. A 0.9 mile walk west along the highway completes the loop, whose total length is just short of 3 miles and takes less than three hours.

96 Peaked Hill and Pond

2.2 miles, 1½ hours from the trailhead on Paradox Lake, 780-foot vertical rise

Ore from the Schofield bed at the head of Paradox Lake supplied a forge at Schroon from 1828 until 1845. Annually it produced 200 tons of the finest bar iron. The pits from the iron mine are visible on private land on the north side of the lake. If you drive along the road north of Paradox at the eastern end of the lake, you will pass a farm with a large charcoal kiln that was never opened. Part of the farmer's fields are full of charcoal.

The trailhead for Peaked Hill lies on the north side of Paradox Lake, reached by canoe from the Paradox Lake Campground. The campground, which is 4.2 miles east of Northway Exit 28 on NY 74, charges a day use fee for launching a boat between May and September. The campground is a great place to stay if you are hiking these hills.

Paddle from the launch site directly north across the lake, rounding the promontory that squeezes the lake into the Narrows. The trailhead is at the eastern end of the Narrows on the north shore, in the first little bay west of the major chain of north shore ledges. Do not expect to find the trailhead marked, for signs keep disappearing. You should see a faint footpath leading north into the woods, and 150 feet along it you should spot a reassuring blue marker.

A short walk and a steep pitch take you under power lines. Beyond, the route continues steeply through second-growth forests, traversing the hillside with a view of the lake through the trees. At 0.25 mile you cross the outlet stream of Peaked Hill Pond. At 0.4 mile the trail levels out. You head west of north through balsam, then birch, walking to the left of a spruce bog. More bog, this one handsome with hemlock, follows at 0.65 mile. The bogs occupy a dip in the height-of-land. The forest becomes deeper and richer with fair-sized hemlock as the trail contours around a small knoll. Big hardwoods, ash, maple, and yellow birch overhang the valley at 0.8 mile. The pond soon becomes visible through the trees and you finish the 1-mile walk to the pond in a beautiful, open, hemlock woods.

The trail turns left to follow the shore west. Shortly it approaches the water, and there is a view across the pond, filtered by hemlock and cedar branches, of Peaked Hill. You continue above the water through the contemplative, quiet woods, winding on a ledge above the pond, through the hemlock into a birch forest at the northern end of the pond. At 1.3 miles, you leave the pond, walking on a ledge through thinner forests of mixed hardwoods.

At 1.5 miles, the trail heads up through a draw where high ground on both sides is covered with white birch. Ledges continue sharply on the right as the trail rounds a little knoll and dips to cross an intermittent stream at 1.5 miles. You follow the west side of the stream, cross the seep from which it flows, and discover you are dependent on the trail markers to follow the trail. There is so little use that at times no foot tread is visible. Beyond the seep you climb again, with charcoal littering the trail. Tremendous fires consumed this ridge.

An hour from the trailhead, at 1.8 miles, you make a sharp turn right, then pass a large glacial erratic. Watch for maidenhair and rattlesnake ferns, and a stand of unusually large long beech ferns. Now you are climbing very steeply and the trail is a bit muddy through the lovely draw. At 1.9 miles you turn to the east toward the summit knob. You pass the trunk of a huge burned pine and climb at 2 miles through scrub pine that are helping reclaim the summit.

New growth has almost restricted views from the north end of the sum-

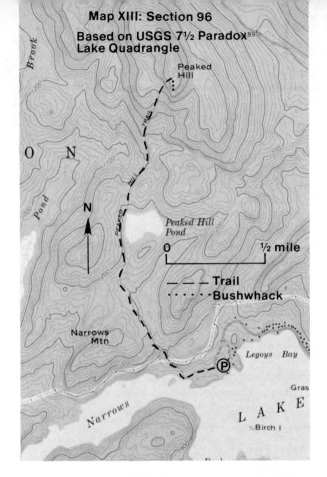

Peaked Hill

Peaked Hill Pond

N

0   ½ mile

— — — Trail
· · · · Bushwhack

Narrows Mtn

P

Legoys Bay

Gras

L A K E

Narrows

Birch I

mit knob, making a fall or early spring climb most desirable. When the leaves are off, or if you explore the summit for openings, you can have limited views in all directions. The range of the High Peaks lies between the north end of Hoffman and Owl Pate mountains.

From the southern end of the summit ridge, you can look down the entire length of Schroon Lake. Peaked Hill Pond is right below you in a line with the Narrows on Paradox Lake. Crane and Huckleberry mountains present a most impressively rugged contour beyond the foot of Schroon Lake. Eleventh Mountain, Gore, and Moxham lead around to the Blue Ridge Range, of which Hoffman Mountain is the central peak. Pharaoh is most obvious to the south and overwhelms the other peaks of that Wilderness.

A word of caution: the road on the north side of Paradox Lake leads to a parking area not 0.2 mile east of the trailhead. The route ahead is private land and parking is restricted, so use the approach by water to the trailhead.

Moriah Road

ESSEX COUNTY ROUTE 4, locally known as the Moriah Road, connects North Hudson and Moriah. The western half of the road bisects a Wild Forest Area, and paths leading from the road reach a number of interior ponds. Those to the north of the road are described in *Discover the Northeastern Adirondacks;* those to the south are in this chapter.

If you drive east on Boreas or Blue Ridge Road toward the Northway, you notice an intriguing cliff-faced mountain rising to the east of the Northway. Bushwhacks from one of this chapter's ponds will take you to that summit, Owl Pate, and to its near twin, Bald Pate.

The area's history parallels regions farther south in Essex County. Timber, principally pine, was harvested from the eastern slopes of the area and taken to Lake Champlain for shipment north to Canada. Logs from the western sections were floated south on the Schroon River to the Hudson River and eventually to Glens Falls.

In 1859, Edgar Burhans took over a tannery on the Schroon River near North Hudson and enlarged it to handle 30,000 hides of sole leather annually. The hides, brought from South America, were shipped up the Hudson, through the Champlain Canal to Crown Point, and then carried by team the nineteen miles to the tannery. This route implies that some of the trails described in this chapter were once part of the connecting roads.

It is also known that wood was harvested from this region for charcoal for the forges and furnaces of Ironville.

As in the areas farther south, fires played a significant role. Today, much of the area is covered with tall pines that pioneered between 100 and 150 years ago on the sandy, fire ravaged soils. Some truly significant forests are encountered, but fire danger persists here because of the dry, sandy soils and the thick carpets of needles covering them. A local ranger has stated that this area has an unusually high potential for fire as well as an unusual attractiveness for hikers. But, so far, few people other than fishermen reach the ponds. The paths are unmarked; even one that was at one time designated as a snowmobile trail is no longer maintained as such. However, the Unit Management Plan for the area calls for marking as trails

Bass Lake

the unmarked paths to Berrymill Flow, Mud Ponds, and both routes to Bass Lake. However, until this is done the beginnings of all the unmarked paths will remain unmarked. They are scattered and concealed along the highways north and east of North Hudson. Take Northway Exit 29 east for 0.3 mile to NY 9, then north 1.4 miles where you bear right at an intersection marked for Port Henry. The path to Bass Lake is at the mid-point of that 0.3 mile segment. All other paths begin from points in the first 5.5 miles of County Route 4.

97 Bass Lake

Path, hiking, cross-country skiing, snowshoeing, fishing, camping

An old logging road to Bass Lake was designated as a snowmobile trail until 1979. Fishermen continue to use the path along the roadway, which makes an excellent trail for all season use. Its future marking and main-tenance as a foot trail will be welcome. It takes but forty-five minutes to cover the 1.6-miles, 400-foot climb to the lake.

To find the beginning, look for a section of the old macadam road lead-ing east from the bypass loop to County Route 4, 0.15 mile east of NY 9. The macadam road once lead to a bridge over Black Brook, but now it ends within 100 feet, near an intersection with the abandoned logging road that heads east. The path along the roadway follows Black Brook past a dam, through a lovely hemlock-and cedar-filled valley.

At 0.25 mile, the path begins to climb away from the valley through a lovely deep woods. Past vehicular use has left the dirt road washed and rutted and occasionally muddy. The ascent continues steadily until at 1 mile you see ledges on the right. For nearly 0.5 mile you cross a relatively level draw through deep, quiet woods with truly big hemlocks. At 1.5 mile you see the lake through the trees and a short descent beneath deep hem-lock covered slopes brings you to the shoreline. People have used this first approach to the lake for camping.

Open rocky ledges are visible along the north shore. Those at the west-ern end of the pond are fairly small and lead to other campsites, but small cliffs rise from the western end. A fisherman's boat may be tied up at shore, and it is obvious that most people have used boats to reach the camping spots, for only rudimentary paths can be found on the shores and even these are not visible all the time.

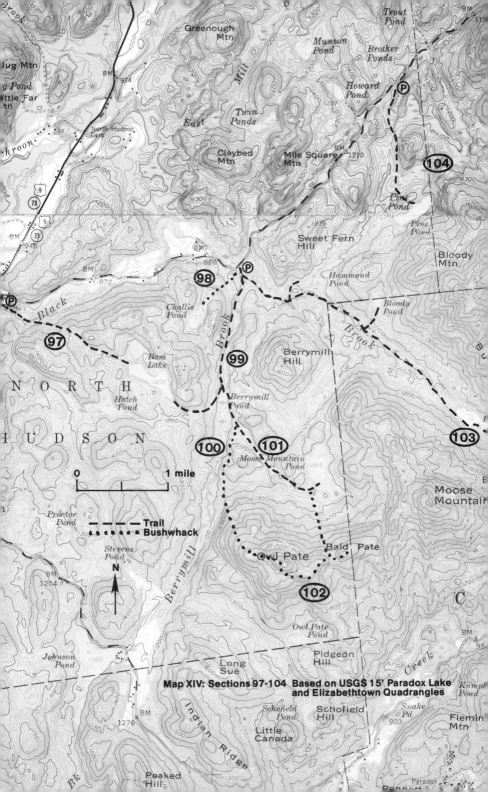

Map XIV: Sections 97-104 Based on USGS 15' Paradox Lake
and Elizabethtown Quadrangles

98 Challis Pond
Short path, hiking, snowshoeing, fishing

An easy-to-follow, unmarked path leads to Challis Pond. The only problem is locating its beginning. If you drive east on the Moriah Road from NY 9, you cross Black Brook at 2.85 miles. In the 0.25 mile before or west of the bridge, three unmarked paths head south. The first, the westernmost, leads to Challis, but has no roadside parking, so it is best to drive to the easternmost and walk back along the road. A tote road 0.1 mile west of the bridge is the route to Hammond Pond. It is marked with a huge pile of chipped bark and there is parking on the side of the tote road near the highway. The path to Challis Pond is 150 yards to the west, beyond a second, smaller turnout.

Challis Pond derives its name from an early pioneer, one Timothy Chellis, who lived two miles east of the Burhans Tannery.

The path leads in 0.6 mile to the pond and takes but twenty minutes to walk. A gentle uphill most of the way, climbing only 200 feet, the path heads southwest, then south to the crest of a small rise at 0.5 mile within sight of the pond. You walk southeast down a moderate grade to the northeast corner of this small, pretty, and secluded pond. You will find many charred tree trunks here. A path, sometimes discernible, sometimes faint, and sometimes lost entirely, leads all around the pond. The shore is covered with hemlock and cedar interspersed with a few white pine, birch, and maple. Waterlilies and pickerel weed mark the shallows of the pond.

99 Berrymill Pond
Path, hiking, snowshoeing, cross-country skiing

The beginning of the path to Berrymill Pond is 0.15 mile west of the bridge over Black Brook and just west of the tote road that leads to Hammond Flow. The latter is distinguished by a bark pile and has parking adjacent to it, near the highway. West of the Hammond Pond tote road you will see a small turnout with no paths leading from it. The path to Berrymill Pond is at the second turnout to the west where there is limited parking.

The path, which will be marked as a foot trail, follows an old tote road. It heads due south through a mixed forest of conifers and yellow birch. Within ten minutes, 0.35 mile, you reach a marsh that lies to the east of the roadway. It is filled with many standing dead trees, the forest of stumps that tells of beaver work. The path continues south wedged between the edge of the marsh and slopes to the west, crossing recent corduroy work on the low spots. Wheel ruts are deep in the mud.

Beyond the marsh, at 0.6 mile, the path climbs at a gentle grade through mixed forests along Berrymill Brook. At 0.9 mile, after about a twenty-five minute walk, you will pass a small waterfall on the brook. The path now climbs a short rise to a height-of-land over a rocky section where you may spot hornblende in the rocks along the way. The height-of-land is 1.25 miles and about thirty-five minutes from the highway.

At the bottom of the short downgrade that follows, you will see a grove of large cedars on the left. A slight upgrade leads to a small clearing with raspberries. The road seems to end at a good campsite in the pines immediately beyond the clearing. Berrymill Pond lies to the south. However, it is no longer really a pond, but a wide marshy area with grasses, alders, and shrubs, stretching west of south for 1.6 miles. In the nineteenth century, a flood dam at the outlet could back up water the entire length of the flow, but now the decayed beaver dam at the outlet raises water level only enough to create channels up to 30 feet in width. At one time, a road beside the flow led all the way south to the vicinity of Johnson Pond, but the route is now too overgrown to be found.

The best way to enjoy the flow is on snowshoes or cross-country skis. The trek to the flow is 1.4 miles long, climbs but 140 feet, and takes forty minutes. In winter you can ski or snowshoe almost a mile and a half down the flow, making a 6 mile round trip to the head of the flow that is suitable for novice skiers.

100 Bass Lake from the East

Path, hiking, fishing, cross-country skiing, snowshoeing

A faint path leads from the Berrymill Flow path to Bass Lake, opening up the possibility for a through trip, especially in winter. The trek adds 0.8 mile, 160 feet vertical rise, and a half hour to the trek to Berrymill Flow, section 99. Whether or not you return via the same route, add this to an exploration of Berrymill Flow, or ski or snowshoe across the frozen waters of Bass Lake and go out via the downhill run of section 97, this makes a good link in a winter day trek, though grades in the link give this an intermediate rating for skiers. In summer, the through route requires a combination of bushwhacking and following fishermen's paths along the shore of Bass Lake. The Unit Management Plan not only calls for marking the route from Berrymill Flow, it also calls for a foot trail along the south side of Bass Lake connecting with the trail to be marked from the west.

The only current problem is that it is hard to find the place the path leaves Berrymill Flow. The fork is located on the west side of the roadway on the downgrade from the height-of-land, north of the grove of cedars. It may be easier to find if you go to the raspberry clearing where a path of sorts leads out to the west end and down through some low areas, quickly intersecting the old road in the vicinity of the path to Bass Lake.

After you find the path, you will discover that it is well defined. It heads southwest, climbing moderately up the flank of a small hill, the slopes of which are covered with a stand of large pine.

The path fords an intermittent stream, then angles west and starts to loop around the hillside. Next it crosses a small bog, and the route beyond this point may be flagged with pink surveyor's ribbons, though these are not high enough to be seen in deep snow. The flagged path starts to angle northwest at the height-of-land as it enters a beautiful, open hemlock forest. Countless moss-covered rocks will trip you up, and the path becomes very hard to follow. Then the ribbons disappear. The land ahead and to the left is relatively level; to the right it slopes uphill fairly steeply. Continue gently uphill, hugging the slopes, bearing right to take a northwesterly course. Then continue northwest to descend toward the lake, arriving at its southernmost bay.

Rock ledges and small cliffs line the east shore in a red pine grove. There are fine views of the lake from the tops of the ledges. A path on the north shore that takes you to the highest ledges disappears quickly. The lake is deep and cold, with very good trout fishing.

There is a fisherman's path heading southeast from the eastern bay. It, too, disappears in blowdowns, but a course of southeast from its discernible end should take you to the mossy hemlock forest where you can spot the ribbons again. The path is relatively easy to follow from here on for the return to the cedar grove near the Berrymill path. Just before you reach the cedars, you may spot an old stone foundation.

101 Moose Mountain Ponds
Path, hiking, fishing

An informal path leads 1.6 miles southeast from Berrymill Pond to Moose Mountain Ponds and adds but 190 feet vertical rise. It adds about forty-five minutes to the Berrymill Pond trek, making a one-way total of an hour and a half for the 3 mile trek. Future marking as a foot trail will generally follow the current path.

At the outlet of Berrymill Pond, section 99, 1.4 miles from Moriah Road, two small logs have been positioned to steady the crossing over wet rocks. A fisherman's path leads along the east shore of the pond, back in the trees, 30 yards or so. With a three minute walk, about 250 yards, beyond the outlet, you pass a rock ledge on your left. Here you will begin to see the charred stumps of large trees that fill the lower reaches of the valley.

The path parallels the pond, and shortly you have an opening right with a pleasant view of the pond and an old beaver lodge. At 0.4 mile, you cross an intermittent stream where to the left a blowdown tree obscures the cutoff to Moose Mountain Pond path. This is a critical turn and has no really distinguishing landmarks, except that if you miss the turn, you will find the path that parallels Berrymill Flow has become much less distinct.

The cutoff runs up the creek bed between two rises in a southeast direction. After a short rise it is almost level as it passes through open woods. A good foot tread is visible. To the right along the flat area there are boulders and a stand of large white pine with two-and-a-half-foot trunks.

At 1 mile, the path forks briefly. The way left is a shortcut, and shortly after the paths rejoin, you reach a major fork. The way left seems to disappear in an open marsh to the northeast. The way right continues southeast up along a hillside and the first steep pitch. This levels off in a marshy low area where through the trees you can look at the ridge between Bald and Owl Pate. The path takes a more easterly direction and winds through a beautiful stand of hemlock and white pine, here with diameters ranging up to three feet. You can see Moose Mountain Pond outlet brook about 30 yards away, and shortly you reach the outlet, a pretty place with rocks showing above the surface of the lily pad and pickerel weed filling the water.

The path follows the west shore to a campsite where there are frames of old lean-tos. You look across from here to Moose Mountain on the east. A faint path wanders north around the west side past several ledge lookouts with good views of the pond. At the far north end there is a large boulder with a vertical face plunging into the water.

102 Bald Pate and Owl Pate
Bushwhack

An exciting bushwhack challenges you to the cliffs on both Bald Pate and Owl Pate, two mountains formed of the anorthosite base typical of the

High Peaks of the Adirondacks. It requires 4.5 miles on a bushwhack loop on top of a walk from the Moriah Road to Berrymill Pond, section 99, and on to Moose Mountain Ponds, section 101, and back. The 9.3 mile trek described will take seven hours.

There are other ways to reach the summits, and in fact a more direct approach to Owl Pate might be desirable, but the bushwhack described here has the advantage of reaching both summits in a circuit. The final approach to the cliffs on Owl Pate is from the south, past ledges that look up at the cliffs on the summit knob.

From the outlet of Moose Mountain Pond, take a bearing of 175° magnetic and follow it up to the upper reaches of the ridge. Continue on the compass course through a mature hardwood forest with specimen examples of yellow birch, ash, and sugar maple. Beech deadfalls from the dieback make sticking to the compass course a bit difficult.

The going gets pretty rough, with the deadfalls, loose, rough footing, and the ever steepening slopes. If you avoid the temptation to follow creek beds and stick to your course, you will reach a draw that leads up to a notch on the ridge or saddle connecting Bald with a hogback of Owl Pate. It will take about an hour to reach the ridge line from Moose Mountain Ponds.

Cliffs lie directly east on the summit knob of Bald Pate. You can attempt to scramble up the cliffs, or continue around the base of the cliffs to the east to scale the knob from the east or, easiest of all, head out of the draw just before, north of, the saddle and scramble up the knob from the north. The routes up the cliffs, with cedar and birch for handholds, are for those who really like rock climbing.

The cliffs are about sixty to one hundred feet high with nice blueberry filled ledges along the top. From Bald Pate you can see Moose Mountain Pond, and to the northeast you can see Bass Lake, with a good view of the High Peaks on the horizon between them. In the south you can see the Pharaoh Lake area, with Pharaoh Mountain quite obvious. To the west, Owl Pate rises formidably. The latter's views are to the south and west, partially screening off the High Peaks, so Bald Pate's views are definitely worth seeking.

To walk to Owl Pate from Bald Pate, choose the easier eastern slopes to descend from Bald Pate, then circle west along Bald Pate's south face, staying fairly close to the base of the cliffs, until you reach the high point of the saddle between the two knobs.

Studying the map would make it seem that your best bet would be to

head up the hogback ridge, which lies toward magnetic west from the ridge. This leads to very steep ledges, so an alternate may be desirable.

Probably the easiest course, one that will lead you past two sets of cliff tops on Owl Pate, requires a southwest course from the saddle, dropping down 200 feet or so in elevation to contour around to the long shoulder of Owl Pate that extends southeast from the summit. If you continue the southwest course, you emerge on the ridge line about 200 feet below the south facing cliffs. Walk parallel to the ridge line, back in the open forest, until you spot the best cliff-top opening.

From these cliffs you have a great view south: Flemmings, Owl Pate, and Johnson ponds, a sliver of Paradox Lake, the Pharaoh Lake Wilderness Area, and a spectacular shot of Knob Mountain. You look the length of Schroon Lake Valley toward Crane Mountain. The view west is blocked by the Blue Ridge and Hoffman mountains.

The south facing cliffs, as well as the ones on Owl Pate's knob, have rounded tops from which the distant views are great, but you cannot look directly down to the valleys below to grasp the scope of their vertical drop. There is no edge as such to look over. The slabs roll away from you until the angle becomes so steep that you may have trouble returning. Watch out!

From a perch on the wonderful rock slabs that slope to the top of the south facing cliffs, you can look north to the cliffs on the west side of Owl Pate's summit knob. To reach those upper cliffs, continue up to the top of the slabs, duck back into open woods, and follow along parallel to the ridge line up to the final knob.

The views from the knob are blocked to the north, and the views south are little more than those from the slab below. However, you can see Sunrise Mountain and part of the Dix Range, and you look directly west up the valley of Blue Ridge Road.

The summit behind is heavily wooded with black spruce. There are almost no openings, just a rare glimpse through the trees.

If you chose the more difficult route from the saddle to Owl Pate's summit via the hogback, you will find that views from the hogback and the easy walk along its ridge line may compensate for the extra effort involved in climbing the hogback's steep eastern ledges.

For this alternate route, head just a little south of west from the saddle, climbing immediately wherever the ledges are not too steep, a 140-foot scramble to the hogback. Contour around the hogback, enjoying views from the southeast through southwest. On the west edge of the hogback you reach a dense spruce thicket. You have to push through it to an area of open hardwood that continues through the saddle between the hogback and Owl Pate. Here stay southwesterly until you reach the ridge line and follow it up the open rock summit area.

To return from Owl Pate, you can follow the long northwest ridge heading down to the foot of Berrymill Flow. This means descending from the knob in a direction of about 285°. The going is quite steep for the first 0.3 mile. In fact you will have to circle small cliffs and ledges. Since the ledges seem to rise in a southeasterly direction, going around to the right will lead you to the shortest drops.

Below the knob, the ridge flattens out slightly for another 0.2 mile, where you walk through an open softwood forest. Your descent is so rapid that this softwood section ends after only a thirty minute walk from the summit. You already start to see again the large burned stumps that are so obvious farther north in the Berrymill Pond valley. To follow the easiest grades, switch your course more northwesterly, about 315°. You may hit a ledge from which you will have a view of Berrymill Flow. If you do, you must angle even more to the north or you will run into more cliffs that are not clearly shown on the maps. Parallel the edge of the escarpment in a northwesterly direction.

After an hour's walk you will complete most of the descent and reach the valley floor. Do not go too far out into the valley or you will reach the alder beds of the flow. Instead, head a little east of north and parallel the valley in the woods. On this descent route, you should hit Berrymill Pond Valley south of Moose Mountain Pond's outlet stream. Walk north for about 0.25 mile to cross the outlet stream as it flows into the valley. From here a very faint path can be followed northward across several small brooks to the junction of the Moose Mountain Pond path. Ahead, to the north, is Berrymill Flow outlet and its beaver dam.

An alternate descent route would be to take a due north heading off Owl Pate's summit to intersect the Moose Mountain Pond outlet brook. Then follow the brook downstream to the valley.

103 Hammond Pond and the Trail upstream along Black Brook

Snowmobile trail, hiking, skiing, fishing
2 miles, 1 hour, 150-foot elevation change

The trail to Hammond Pond and beyond toward Black Brook Ponds follows an old road that is an active snowmobile trail. It leads to private lands

near Black Brook Ponds. The first 2 miles pass through a beautiful deep forest, beside Hammond Pond, and through the valley of Black Brook. You will find it a lovely nature trail and an excellent novice ski trail, if you watch out for snowmobiles.

The trail follows an old tote road that heads southeast from the Moriah Road, less than 0.1 mile west of the bridge over Black Brook and 2.8 miles east of NY 9. This is the road marked with a large pile of bark. There is a fork near the beginning, and the way right goes nowhere. You head left along the jeep road on which you will discover four-wheel-drive vehicles have driven all the way to the pond.

A short downhill leads to a ford over Berrymill Brook. Beyond it, the road turns southeast, briefly uphill, then levels off in a forest of very large white pine. It is nice to walk along the roadway here, for the needle carpet is thick and spongy.

You pass a red pine plantation on the right, with the marshes around Black Brook now visible on the left and the ledges on Sweet Fern Hill visible to the east. A great variety of ferns borders the roadway, and in late summer mushrooms add bright patches of white to the forest floor.

After a twenty minute walk, 0.75 mile, the roadway forks. The left fork leads in 0.1 mile to a campsite at the outlet. Across it, to the north, are 50-foot cliffs on Sweet Fern Hill.

The pond is shallow, with warm water species of fish. The shallows make the pond most attractive; there are frogs and snakes and rotten logs. The water is nearly filled with pickerel weed, water lilies, and water chinquapin, *Nelumbo lutea*, a lotus-like weed. White and paper birch line the shoreline. You may see great blue heron and many kinds of ducks. Overhanging the pond to the east are the slopes of Hail Mountain, whose northern summit is called Bloody Mountain, while the fire-scarred and open ledges on the south form the Burnt Ridges. Even if you do not fish, you will certainly enjoy the pond better from a canoe or inflatable boat.

From the fork, the way right, southeast, leads uphill to a ridge above the south shore that you follow for 0.5 mile. There are views of the pond and its marshes through the trees. You leave the southeastern corner of the pond and follow the inlet, crossing it in 0.1 mile at 1.35 miles via an old plank bridge. A little over 0.1 mile beyond, you cross a stream flowing from your left on a second plank bridge. It is the outlet of Bloody Pond, and a path marked with yellow paint follows the east side of the outlet stream to the pond, a distance of 0.25 mile. That tiny teardrop also attracts fishermen.

Hammond Pond

A detour uphill will take you to the pond in 10 minutes. The path is rocky all the way to the pond, where you will find a sportsman's path going around the pond to the right. It passes several lookouts, fire rings, and duck hunter's blinds.

The roadway and its snowmobile trail along Black Brook continue southeast, crossing again to the south side of the brook 0.1 mile past the turn to Bloody Pond. The roadway continues beside a small pond and a string of marshes along the brook before reaching private land at 2 miles, at a point immediately north of Black Brook Pond.

104 Pine Pond
Bushwhack

The hike to Pine Pond starts out along an old logging road that gradually deteriorates and becomes difficult to follow. The last 0.4 mile to the pond must be considered a bushwhack, so you should not attempt this trip unless you are skilled with the use of map and compass.

Pine Pond is a really handsome place with high, dry shores suitable for camping. There is supposed to be good pike fishing.

To find the logging road, drive east from NY 9 on the Moriah Road for 5.5 miles to the town line monument, then continue east for 0.25 mile. Look for a large birch about 10 to 15 feet from the road. It has an old blaze and marks the beginning of the logging road, which is headed south.

Walk south along the road and immediately cross a wet area that is the start of a brook shown on the USGS map as running parallel with the roadway. The roadway takes a course of 200° through a stand of medium-sized hemlock and balsam, with the brook on the right, west, and a steep hill on the left, east. Thick alders border the brook, which swings away to the west and stays out of sight. The roadway traverses low ground and then, at about 0.3 mile, climbs through a small notch in a southerly direction into a stand of larger balsam and pine.

After fifteen minutes of walking, there is a slight rise in the roadway into an area covered with good sized red pines. A descent leads, at 0.5 mile, about a twenty minute walk, to a large brook, which you cross without benefit of a bridge. As you begin to climb on the opposite side there are many large pines. The roadway turns west of south again to follow the brook valley. The roadway, which bears a few old blazes, continues at about 200° magnetic generally downhill again.

At 1 mile, a thirty-five minute walk, you reach a low area thick with balsam. Here you cross a very small brook. On the south side of the low area there is a large blaze pointing the way to higher ground. Continue a little west of south, still following the brook valley for another 0.2 mile. By now almost all signs of the roadway have disappeared. If you cannot follow the fading footpath, the easiest thing to do is to leave the valley and turn sharply southeast and uphill for a ten to fifteen minute, 0.4 mile, bushwhack to the northern shore of the pond. This route avoids a large wet area near the pond's outlet where a beaver meadow is filling with young white pine. It could make wet walking. The suggested route keeps you to the north side of this area and south of a second swamp. The last 0.25 mile is uphill to the shore of the pond. The entire 1.6 mile walk with its net descent of 160 feet should take about an hour if you allow for searching for the roadway and the proper course.

The pond is beautiful with mountains on the east side dropping directly down to water level. You will find many good camping possibilities along the high ground on the northwest side of the pond. The vistas across the water are especially nice.

To return to the roadway, reverse your bushwhack course, using the sharp hill west of the brook as a visual guide to intersect the roadway on the east side of the brook valley.

References and Other Resources

Alling, Harold L. *Adirondack Graphite Deposits.* Albany, New York: New York State Museum, 1918.

Brown, William H., editor. *History of Warren County.* New York: Board of Supervisors of Warren County, 1963.

Emmons, Ebenezer. New York State Geological Report, 1842.

Loescher, Burt Garfield. *The History of Rogers Rangers, Volume I.* San Francisco: printed by the author, 1946.

Mason, Howard C. *Backward Glances, Vol. I.* Privately printed.

Newland, D. H., and Vaughn, Henry. *Guide to the Geology of Lake George.* Albany, New York: The University of the State of New York, 1942.

New York State Department of Environmental Conservation Brochures:
Adirondack Wilderness Guide to Pharaoh Lake Area Map
Horse Trails in New York State
Lake George
Snowmobile Trails in New York State
Trails in the Lake George Region
Trails in the Schroon Lake Region

New York State Department of Environmental Conservation. *Unit Management Plans* or *Draft Plans* for *Pharaoh Lake Wilderness, Hammond Pond Wild Forest, Bald Ledge* and *Crane Pond Primitive Areas, Black Mountain portion of the Lake George Wild Forest.*

New York State Joint Legislative Committee on Lake George Water Conditions. *Lake George.* New York State Legislature, 1945.

Ogilvie, Ida H. *Geology of the Paradox Lake Quadrangle, New York.* Albany, New York, The New York State Museum, 1905.

Ross, W. C. *History of Graphite New York.* Glens Falls, New York: Ridgcraft Books, 1971.

Smith, H. P., editor. *History of Essex County.* Syracuse: Essex County, 1855.

Steinback, Elsa Kny. *Sweet Peas and a White Bridge.* Sylvan Beach, New York: North Country Books, 1974.

Stiles, Fred Tracy. *From Then Til Now.* New York, Washington County Historical Society, 1978.

Towson, Charles A. *The Story of a Hamlet Called Paradox*. Privately printed.
Van de Water, Frederic F. *Lake Champlain and Lake George*. Port Washington, New York: Ira J. Friedman, Inc., 1969. (Reprint of 1946 edition.)
Watson, Winslow C. *Military and Civil History of the County of Essex*. Albany, New York: J. Munsell, 1869.

Maps and Atlases:
    Burr's Atlas Essex County, 1840.
    Grey's Atlas Essex County, 1876.
    Beer's Atlas Warren County, 1876.
    U. S. Geological Survey Topological Maps, 1895 series.

Other Resources

Adirondack Mountain Club, Glens Falls, New York, 12801
Department of Environmental Conservation, 50 Wolf Road, Albany, New York, 12233. Region 5, Regional Office, Warrensburg, New York
Lake George Association, Box 408, Fort George Road, Lake George, New York, 12845

To find your way around back roads:
    Adirondack Atlas, City Street Directory, Poughkeepsie, New York, $3.75

For more information
    Adirondack North Country Regional Map
    Citizen's Guide to the Adirondack Forest Preserve
       Both are available from the Adirondack Park Agency, Box 99, Ray Brook, New York, 12977

Index

Guidebooks from Backcountry Publications

State Parks and Campgrounds

State Parks and Campgrounds in Northern New York, by John Scheib $9.95

Walks and Rambles Series

Walks and Rambles on the Delmarva Peninsula, by Jay Abercrombie $8.95

Walks and Rambles in Westchester (NY) and Fairfield (CT) Counties, by Katherine Anderson $7.95

Walks and Rambles in Rhode Island, by Ken Weber $8.95

Biking Series

25 Bicycle Tours in New Jersey, by Arline and Joel Zatz $8.95

25 Bicycle Tours on Delmarva, by John Wennersten $8.95

25 Bicycle Tours in Maine, by Howard Stone $8.95

25 Bicycle Tours in Vermont, by John Freidin $7.95

25 Bicycle Tours in New Hampshire, by Tom and Susan Heavey $6.95

20 Bicycle Tours in the Finger Lakes, by Mark Roth and Sally Waters $7.95

20 Bicycle Tours in and around New York City, by Dan Carlinsky and David Heim $6.95

25 Bicycle Tours in Eastern Pennsylvania, by Dale Adams and Dale Speicher $7.95

Canoeing Series

Canoe Camping Vermont and New Hampshire Rivers, by Roioli Schweiker $6.95

Canoeing Central New York, by William P. Ehling $9.95

Canoeing Massachusetts, Rhode Island and Connecticut, by Ken Weber $7.95

Hiking Series

50 Hikes in New Jersey, by Bruce Scofield *et al.* $10.95

50 Hikes in the Adirondacks, by Barbara McMartin $9.95

50 Hikes in Central New York, by William P. Ehling $8.95

50 Hikes in the Hudson Valley, by Barbara McMartin and Peter Kick $9.95

50 Hikes in Central Pennsylvania, by Tom Thwaites $9.95

50 Hikes in Eastern Pennsylvania, by Carolyn Hoffman $9.95

50 Hikes in Western Pennsylvania, by Tom Thwaites $9.95

50 Hikes in Maine, by John Gibson $8.95

50 Hikes in the White Mountains, by Daniel Doan $9.95

50 More Hikes in New Hampshire, by Daniel Doan $9.95

50 Hikes in Vermont, 3rd edition, revised by the Green Mountain Club $9.95

50 Hikes in Massachusetts, by John Brady and Brian White $9.95

50 Hikes in Connecticut, by Gerry and Sue Hardy $8.95

50 Hikes in West Virginia, by Ann and Jim McGraw $9.95

The above titles are available at bookstores and at certain sporting goods stores or may be ordered directly from the publisher. For complete descriptions of these and other guides, write: Backcountry Publications, P.O. Box 175, Woodstock, VT 05091.

Edythe Robbins has lived in New York all her life, first in Ithaca and now in Hudson Falls. She began exploring at the age of three and hasn't been able to stop since. She has explored on foot, skis, snowshoes, bicycle, and canoe and cannot easily ignore a back road, fisherman's path, meandering stream, or an open summit. Edythe has climbed all of the 4000-foot peaks in the Adirondacks and is a member of the 46ers. Because she lives near the area covered by this guide, it was easy for her to re-check many of the trails for this revised edition. She also added new information on the Pilot Knob area. Edythe contributed to *Discover the Central Adirondacks* and will be assisting in future "Discover" series guides.

Photo by Barbara McMartin

A00015000008782